By
Request

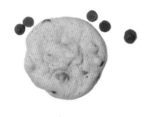

CRAIG T. KOJIMA

Star ★ Bulletin

BY
REQUEST

The Search for Hawai'i's
Greatest Recipes

BETTY SHIMABUKURO

MUTUAL PUBLISHING

The recipes, stories, and photographs in this cookbook are reprinted with the permission of the *Honolulu Star-Bulletin*.

Library of Congress Cataloging-in-Publication Data

Shimabukuro, Betty.
  By request : the search for Hawaii's greatest recipes / Betty Shimabukuro.
    p. cm.
  Summary: "A cookbook of memorable, favorite, and popular recipes based on the Honolulu Star-Bulletin's By Request column by Betty Shimabukuro. This collection of local recipes include old favorites grandma used to make to unique dishes found at local restaurants"--Provided by publisher.
  Includes index.
  ISBN 1-56647-773-5 (pbk. : alk. paper)
  1. Hawaiian cookery. I. Title.
  TX724.5.H3.S54 2006
  641.59969--dc22
                    2006007020

ISBN-10: 1-56647-773-5
ISBN-13: 978-1-56647-773-4

Design by Leo Gonzalez

First Printing, April 2006
Second Printing, May 2006
Third Printing, February 2007
Fourth Printing, November 2007

Mutual Publishing, LLC
1215 Center Street, Suite 210
Honolulu, Hawai'i 96816
Ph: 808-732-1709 / Fax: 808-734-4094
Email: info@mutualpublishing.com
www.mutualpublishing.com

Printed in Korea

Table of Contents

DENNIS ODA

DENNIS ODA

TOP PHOTOS AND BOTTOM RIGHT PHOTO
BY DENNIS ODA, BOTTOM LEFT PHOTO BY KATHRYN BENDER

Introduction

This cookbook is a collection of excerpts from the *Honolulu Star-Bulletin*'s "By Request" column, a regular part of the newspaper's Wednesday Food section. The concept is simple: Readers write in for recipes and I try to find them.

Their requests run from the most elaborate restaurant dishes to shoyu hot dogs, from contemporary trendy foods to old favorites from drive-ins that closed long ago.

"By Request" predates my tenure at the *Star-Bulletin* by many years. I took it over late in 1998, even though at the time the most you could say about my cooking ability was that I had a stove and I wasn't afraid to use it. As such it is the generosity and skill of many, many Hawai'i chefs, home cooks, and cooking teachers who really make "By Request" possible week after week.

I know from my own use of cookbooks that most people just want to find their recipes and get out. Sorry, but this cookbook is a collection of stories as much as recipes—I've found that many times the search for a recipe and the story behind it is as interesting as the dish itself.

Curiosity fuels *By Request* as much as hunger. Happy cooking.

Betty Shimabukuro
Food and Features editor,
Honolulu Star-Bulletin

Top Five Requests

Some recipe requests will never be granted, because the people who hold the secret formulas just won't let them out.

Others are elusive because the chef or restaurant disappeared long ago, or because the recipe itself is a mystery.

These five recipes had reached legendary status in my files and those of my predecessors. Earnest cooks had been seeking them for years. Good timing and good luck finally brought them to light.

February 9, 2005

Alice Yang—better known as Chicken Alice—was famous in the 1980s and '90s for her slightly spicy, very crispy chicken wings. But after her restaurant closed in 1995, those beloved wings disappeared.

The Chicken Alice recipe was a top reader request for years. A typical plea: "They had THE BEST spicy Korean chicken wings that were virtually red with all the chili peppers. I really miss those chicken wings!"

Well, early in 2005, someone recognized her at her current place of work, a bar called Club Star Palace, where she's the manager, and called me. I called her. She said, "Okay."

Alice came to Hawaiʻi from Seoul thirty years ago as a college student with an interest in business. She started with a bar near the University of Hawaiʻi, then in 1980 opened the Korea House bar on Keʻeaumoku Street, in the land mass now occupied by Wal-Mart.

Although her mother owned a restaurant in Seoul, Alice didn't build up a cooking background. "I never thought I was going to

F.L. MORRIS

have a restaurant. I guess it's destiny. Or fate."

But she wanted a finger food she could give her customers—thus were her famous chicken wings born, the perfect accompaniment to cocktails.

The wings proved immensely popular, so, in 1982, Alice opened a restaurant in their honor, Chicken Alice's on Kapi'olani Boulevard just outside Ala Moana Center. She sold takeout Korean dishes, too, but it was the wings that cemented her success.

When she closed the restaurant in 1995, a long dry spell began for her fans.

But Alice says she's ready to share the recipe, in return for the warmth that she's received since moving here. "I give it away to state of Hawai'i people," she says. "I hope they like it."

The wings are battered in a simple mixture of flour, water, salt, and garlic. The key ingredient is Parks Brand kim chee sauce—made locally and used primarily as a base for kim chee. It includes chili peppers, fish sauce, paprika, garlic, and ginger—and turns the batter pink.

"We buy from the factory, by the bucket, 5 gallons," Alice says of her restaurant days.

The sauce is available in Asian groceries—if you want to be sure to find it, go to a Korean market such as Pālama Super Market. Look for it in the refrigerated section, near the kim chee and tofu.

The recipe is simple, but technique counts for a lot. By that I mean skillful deep-frying. Alice's wings are nice and crunchy on the outside, juicy and perfectly cooked inside. If you don't fry a lot, you'll probably have patchy results until you get the hang of it. Oil temperature needs to be a consistent 350°F so you don't burn the outside before the inside is cooked through.

Chicken Alice's Wings

Serves 12 to 15

5 pounds chicken wings
 Vegetable oil for deep-frying (Wesson brand preferred)

Batter:

⅓ cup Parks Brand kim chee sauce
1 tablespoon minced garlic
2 tablespoons salt
2½ cups flour
2 cups water, or more, as needed

Rinse and dry chicken. Cut off and discard wing tips. Cut through joint to separate drummettes from other half of wing.

To make Batter: Combine kim chee sauce, garlic, salt, and flour. Add water gradually, enough to make a thick batter.

Add chicken pieces to batter, mix well, and marinate in refrigerator 2 to 3 hours.

Heat oil to 350°F. Deep-fry chicken pieces about 10 minutes, until chicken rises to surface and coating is deep brown.

F.L. MORRIS

April 6, 2005

I've been trying to understand the gravitational attraction of oatcakes, gravity being an apt word as these baked items are dense, heavy, and as solid as planet Earth.

They are also irresistibly chewy and so full of fruit and oatmeal that they reek of good health. Although, how healthy they really are depends on how much butter, sugar, and/or eggs have been added to make all those dry oats palatable.

The center of the oatcake universe is the low-fat version sold at Starbucks coffee houses on O'ahu. Over the years, dozens of readers have asked for this recipe.

The oatcake is made for Starbucks by Honolulu Baking Co. and the recipe is proprietary. There being no constitutional provision forcing Starbucks to give it up, you can all stop asking.

The oatcake is a 2-inch cube in a bizarre shade of dark gray. "It's not the most pretty of pastries," Sherri Rigg, Starbucks Hawai'i's marketing director, admits. But customers are quite faithful to it.

The cake has a nice, chewy texture and is not too sweet. As for what makes it that color, or what exactly is in it—well, that's proprietary, too.

But you can't stop people from trying. Home baker Margo Lynn loves the Starbucks oatcake and was determined to duplicate it. She collaborated with a friend, a retired nutritionist. They came pretty darn close, and whatever's different about their oatcake is for the better. They even got close to the funky gray color of the Starbucks' version, through a blueberry puree.

The nutritional comparison favors Margo: Half of a Starbucks oatcake (yes, you are only supposed to eat half at a time) contains 258 calories, 3.3 grams of fat, and 4.5 grams of fiber. One of Margo's oatcakes, which is about half the size of Starbucks' to begin with, is 220 calories, 2.5 grams fat, 6 grams fiber.

Margo's Low-fat Oatcakes

Makes about 20 squares

2	cups whole-wheat flour
½	teaspoon salt
1	teaspoon baking soda
1	teaspoon cinnamon
½	teaspoon nutmeg
1	cup warm water
½	cup dried blueberries
4	cups rolled oats
1	cup applesauce
½	cup Splenda® (or ½ cup brown sugar)
1	teaspoon vanilla
⅔	cup Egg Beaters® egg substitute (or about 3 eggs)
1	cup dried cranberries
1 ½	cups raisins

Preheat oven to 350°F. Grease and flour a 9 x 13-inch pan.

Sift together flour, salt, and spices.

Put warm water and dried blueberries in a blender and purée (depending on the strength of your blender, you might want to start with 1/2 cup water until the berries are pretty well chopped, then add the rest). Add blueberry purée to oats.

Beat together applesauce, Splenda®, and vanilla. Beat in Egg Beaters®. Stir in oats and flour mixtures. Fold in cranberries and raisins. Press mixture evenly into pan. Sprinkle raw oats on top. Bake 30 minutes, or until cake is cooked in the center. Cool, then cut.

October 25, 1999

Let's say you're a chef. Not the hamburger-flipping kind, but a star chef with your name on a restaurant or two. You spend your evenings crafting elegant meals, layered with sophisticated sauces, topped with delicate garnishes, paired with expensive wines.

Kitchen closes. You could go somewhere soft and refined, relax to soothing music and a nice drink, maybe have a cigar.

Or you could go to a smoky bar, packed with people and noise, where they feed you a big old plate of pork chops. And you can have a cigar.

What do you pick?

Pork chops.

That's the fascinating thing about Side Street Inn, an unassuming, nondescript place in Kaka'ako that just happens to be the favorite hang out of the most accomplished chefs in the islands.

This is where Roy Yamaguchi and Alan Wong, masters of Hawai'i regional cuisine, were singing "Chotto Matte Kudasai" into karaoke microphones very late on a recent Tuesday night, after two (or was it three?) rounds of vodka shots and piles of pork chops, chicken gizzards, fried rice, smoked pork, and sashimi.

The pork chops are a universal favorite, which Side Street owner Colin Nishida was happy to share, but he doesn't write down his recipes or measure, so he'd never officially given it out.

Securing this recipe required standing next to him in the kitchen, writing down everything he threw in the pan and guestimating quantities.

It's close, though.

His secret: Fresh island pork chops.

You can't argue with success.

Side Street Pork Chops

Serves 4

2   tablespoons garlic salt
2   tablespoons pepper
1 ⅓   cups flour
⅔   cup cornstarch
4   7-ounce fresh island pork chops, about 1 inch thick
1   cup cottonseed oil

Combine garlic salt, pepper, flour, and cornstarch. Coat chops well in the mixture. Heat oil in a skillet. Fry chops about 10 minutes, turning frequently until browned.

Cut meat from the bones and slice the chops into bite-sized pieces. Serve over shredded cabbage with ketchup on the side. Include bones for gnawing.

DENNIS ODA

February 9, 2005

The Tahitian Lanai Restaurant hasn't really been gone all that long—it closed on New Year's Eve in 1997—but it was 40 years old and people tended to consider it a historic treasure, one of the last relics of Old Waikīkī.

For Ruby Washington, the Tahitian Lanai was the place her husband headed for everyday at 5:30 a.m. He'd come home— "God knows when," she says. "We're sleeping already."

Anderson Washington was executive chef at the Tahitian Lanai, responsible for many signature dishes that are as beloved as the grass-shack romance of the restaurant itself.

Anderson Washington was from Charlottesville, Va., and trained as a chef in New York, Mrs. Washington says. The couple met in her hometown of Hilo in the 1940s, when he was in the Army. She was a waitress at a Filipino restaurant.

They married and moved to Kāneʻohe in 1950. He took a job with Spencecliff Corp., which eventually would open not just the Tahitian Lanai, but also the Tiki Tops, Queen's Surf, and Fisherman's Wharf restaurants.

Anderson Washington died in 2002 at age 92. Mrs. Washington, now 79, kept her husband's cookbook from the restaurant, as well as a collection of newspaper clippings, recipe cards, and other memorabilia.

When she read that several readers were looking for what was probably her husband's best-loved dish, Moa Ta Haari Chicken, she dug it up.

The dish was served in a coconut half that was kept from rolling around the plate with a stabilizing spoonful of mashed potatoes.

Moa Ta Haari Chicken

Serves 4 to 6

1 ¾ cups milk
1 ¾ cups coconut milk
2 tablespoons chopped celery
2 tablespoons chopped onion
3 whole cloves
1 tablespoon chicken base (see note)
1 tablespoon lemon zest
1 tablespoon salt and white pepper
1 tablespoon cornstarch
18 ounces cooked, diced chicken

Combine milk, coconut milk, celery, onion, cloves, and chicken base in saucepan. Heat slowly, stirring constantly, until boiling. Add zest, salt, and pepper.

Dissolve cornstarch in small amount of cold water to make a paste. Add to saucepan. Cook 10 minutes.

Strain and add chicken. Serve with each portion garnished with hollandaise sauce.

Note: Chicken base is a paste sold in the soup aisle of supermarkets, near the chicken bouillon.

January 21, 2004

Toong mai is a crunchy Chinese puffed-rice cake, sort of like Rice Krispy Treats, but better. It is a favorite of celebrations such as the Lunar New Year, but not often made in the home, for good reason.

The traditional method involves soaking and steaming the rice, drying it in the sun, then making it pop in a wok filled with hot sand. Hot sand. Not a project I was willing to undertake without supervision.

Many readers over the years have asked for this recipe. A few others had copies of recipes, but none had actually made the rice cakes themselves. Three people volunteered that their aunties could make toong mai, but alas, the aunties declined to go public. "Very Asian," one caller said, by way of explanation.

At Shung Chong Yuein, the Chinatown cake shop that sells the best toong mai in town, owner Judy Ng would only say that the rice cakes are made for her by an older woman, using sand.

It seemed toong mai was produced by magic, or perhaps elves. (The above mentioned aunties actually turn into elves to puff their rice, which is why they don't want strangers watching them. Okay, that was a lie, but you can see how this quest was beginning to take on mythical proportions.)

The journey was one of false starts and false hopes, but also of great stories that remind us that food is about history, culture, and shared memories as much as it is about recipes. And on a Wednesday early in the Year of the Monkey, from my kitchen emerged a decently acceptable slab of toong mai. Not as wonderfully crunchy and compact as what you can get in Chinatown, but do I look like your popo?

Toong mai is actually a Hawai'i-only name that doesn't make sense in Chinese, according to "Chinese New Year: Fact and Folklore," by William C. Hu (*Ars Ceramica*, 1991). The original name was chi'ao-mi-kao, and it was brought to Hawai'i by the Hakka people, who shortened the name to mi-ch'ang, probably a combination of mi-kung (sweet cakes) and mi-t'ung (puffed, hollowed-out rice).

Hu described a tedious process: Mochi rice was spread on bamboo trays to dry for half a day. Coarse sand was heated until red hot in a wok, then the dried rice was added by the bowlful to puff. A special utensil was then used to separate rice from sand. Finally, a sugar syrup was boiled, mixed with the rice and some peanuts, and everything was pressed flat.

The key to making toong mai is clearly in the puffing. Hot sand isn't the only way.

In Taiwan, traveling vendors would carry rice-puffing pans that operated something like pressure cookers. They'd puff the rice for all the moms in a neighborhood.

A similar process on a larger scale is used at the Hawai'i Candy Co., where president Keith Ohta describes his rice-puffing machine as "like a cannon." The 6-foot-long chamber pressurizes under heat. The rice goes in and basically explodes out.

You see why no one makes Rice Krispies at home?

That said, toong mai is achieveable at home, just don't expect it to be easy.

Before you begin, check your equipment: You'll need a

steamer, preferably the Chinese bamboo type, cheesecloth, a couple of small pots, a rolling pin, spatula, and a flat, wire-mesh strainer.

Also, check your schedule: Working straight through, this will take most of the day, on top

BETTY SHIMABUKURO

of soaking the rice overnight. You can spread the work out over a couple of days, though.

And, check the weather: Many toong mai recipes suggest that you not attempt this on a humid or rainy day.

Toong Mai

1   cup mochi rice (sweet, glutinous rice)
     Vegetable oil for deep-frying
1   cup water
½   cup sugar
1   teaspoon vinegar
¼   cup dry-roasted peanuts, preferably unsalted

Cover rice in water and soak at least 3 hours, or overnight.

Drain rice. Spread a layer of cheesecloth in the bottom of a steamer basket. Place rice in an even layer over cheesecloth. Cover and steam over boiling water 40 minutes, or until rice is soft. Cool.

Preheat oven to 175°F. Spread rice evenly on a baking sheet (grains will be very sticky, but try to separate as much as possible). Bake 45 minutes. Every 15 minutes turn and separate rice so it dries evenly.

Turn off oven. Leave rice in oven 3 to 4 hours, until completely hard and dry.

Pour about 2 inches of oil into a small pot. Heat to 375°F. Scoop a small amount of dried rice onto strainer and lower into hot oil. The rice will puff and rise. Use strainer to separate and turn rice grains. When rice just starts to color—in a few seconds—lift out with strainer, tapping the side of the pot to shake off excess oil. Drain on paper towels.

Working in small batches, puff the remaining rice. (Don't try to hurry the process by using a larger pot. The rice cooks quickly and will burn if you can't get it out of the pot fast enough.)

Break up any clumps of rice and immediately store in an airtight container. You should have about 4 cups. Discard oil. (If you're tired now, go to bed. Finish in the morning.)

Bring water, sugar, and vinegar to a boil. Simmer until a thick syrup forms and mixture begins to turn light brown, about 30 minutes (240°F to 245°F on a candy thermometer, halfway between soft- and hard-ball).

When syrup is almost ready, combine puffed rice and peanuts in a large, lightly oiled bowl. Oil a spatula and a baking sheet. Pour syrup over rice and stir quickly, using spatula, so rice is evenly coated. Work quickly, as syrup cools and hardens quickly. Spread on baking sheet and form by hand into a 3/4-inch thick layer. Press firmly with a rolling pin to compress to 1/2-inch thickness, pushing in the edges as you go to maintain shape. Cool and cut.

Variations: Grated ginger and sesame seeds may be added to the puffed rice. You can also vary the amount of peanuts and experiment with more or less syrup, depending on how sweet or chewy you like it.

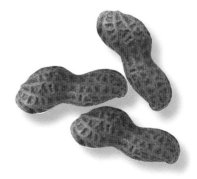

Salads and Sides

Consider Thanksgiving, that world-champion day of eating. The turkey sits there like a crown prince in the center of the table, and yet, the memorable parts of the meal are usually what surround the bird—mom's stuffing or aunty's special mushroom dish.

Salads and side dishes play a supporting role at dinner or on the buffet line, but it is their job to provide color and variety. Without them, it's a meat-and-potatoes world (or meat-and-rice). And who wants to live there?

February 26, 2003

Alan Awana is the new chef at Washington Place, Gov. Linda Lingle's personal guy in the kitchen. It's his food she eats daily and it's his food you'll eat if you're ever invited to a state function at Hawai'i's First House.

Should the governor ever come to your house, here's what you don't want to serve: "Definitely not pickles, any kind of pickles," Awana says. "She doesn't even want to see them on the plate." And she doesn't drink coffee. "She doesn't even care for the aroma when it's brewing."

Other than that, Awana says, she's not picky. "She's just a healthy eater, which is good."

Lingle especially likes salads and beef stew—"hold the mac salad"—and chocolate chip cookies, bite-sized.

Awana comes from a cooking family. His father, Ben E. C. Awana, was in the partnership that opened Ha'ikū Gardens a generation ago. Dad's signature dish: smoked spareribs.

From his own repertoire of no-nonsense cooking comes this poke recipe that he fixes often for parties, although it came out of humble circumstances.

"We were camping and didn't have a lot of ingredients, but we just happened to have a lot of cilantro and a lot of peppers that we were roasting. It's been a hit ever since."

Asian Poke   Serves 24

2	pounds 'ahi, any good grade, cubed
½	cup light olive oil
2	cups soy sauce
6	cloves garlic, minced
4	sweet red jalapeño peppers, deveined, halved lengthwise and cut in thin strips
½	bunch cilantro, 1/4-inch pieces, stems included

Drizzle 'ahi with olive oil and soy sauce. Mix in garlic, peppers, and cilantro; stir well. Serve chilled.

June 22, 2001

Bea Shimabukuro was happy to talk about her post-retirement life and her turkey stuffing—but could it wait a week? She was busy preparing for a big karaoke contest.

Bea's Drive-In having been reborn in April with a new name and new ownership, the Bea of the old marquee is busy with Bible study, church work, exercise classes, and karaoke. And yet, she says, "I still complain that I want to go back to work."

This is what happens when you've been in business forty-seven years, when some of your customers have been around for every one of those years, when you basically love what you do.

But for health considerations and other reasons, Bea (who, by the way, is not related to me—too bad) had to give up her Kaimukī drive-in.

She'd been known for hearty plates of hamburger steak, beef stew, and roast turkey—plus bowls of oxtail and pig's feet soup.

This stuffing, flavored with lots of bacon and margarine, was a particular favorite of her customers. She normally made enough to pair with 50 pounds of turkey, never really measuring. Still, she painstakingly measured out a recipe at home, breaking it down to a more workable amount.

Bea's story begins in 1953, when Bea bought Donald Duck Drive-In. She was just 20 years old and lived in an apartment above the restaurant. The next year, her son was born.

In the early '60s, she tore down the old Donald Duck and put up a new Bea's, the first of four renovations. It was a true drive-in, with carhops.

Earlier this year, Shimabukuro sold her restaurant to Kayoko Kiyoto, who renamed it Kay's Grill and Saimin Stand. Many of Bea's old customers are new patrons of Kay's, as is Bea, who meets there often with various groups of friends.

Bea's Drive-In Turkey Stuffing

	Giblets from 1 turkey
4	cups water
10	slices bacon, diced
1	small onion, diced
4	stalks celery, diced
1	pound margarine
2 ½	tablespoons poultry seasoning, or more to taste
2	24-ounce loaves bread, broken into small pieces
	Dash of salt and pepper

Boil giblets in water until tender; dice. Reserve cooking water.

Fry bacon; when almost crisp add onion and celery. Brown vegetables, then add giblets and margarine. When margarine is melted, add poultry seasoning. Add up to 3 cups of cooking water from giblets, depending on how soft you like your stuffing. Bring to a boil, then reduce heat and simmer 15 minutes.

Toss mixture with bread, then season with salt and pepper.

Note: This is a stove-top stuffing, so it doesn't go in the oven or inside your turkey. It makes more than enough to serve with a large roast turkey. It also can be served as an accompaniment for roast chicken or duck.

March 20, 2002

Anne Yamamoto and son Brian opened the first Yama's twenty-two years ago in Waipahu. At the time she was an office worker and he had a year left of college. "I told him, 'Finish college,' but he said he wanted to open a business."

The market carries all manner of seafoods, including various types of poke, 'opihi, pulehu tako, and dried 'ahi. But, Yamamoto says, "You can't make money only selling fish, so I went into simple foods, like stews."

Now Yama's caters, makes lunch deliveries to businesses around town, and even assembles Hawaiian Care Packages for carrying to homesick college students on the mainland.

At the heart of it all, though, is Yamamoto's "simple food," including laulau, kalua pig, chicken long rice, lomi salmon, and sweet potato/haupia pies.

A customer favorite is Yamamoto's cone sushi, sold at the second Yama's location on Young Street.

She was willing to share this recipe, but no matter how faithful you are to it, yours probably won't quite come up to Yamamoto's level.

Her son says that when she's on vacation, customers complain that the sushi just doesn't taste the same.

Sushi Vinegar

2 ⅔   cups sugar
2 ⅓   cups vinegar
      Pinch of salt
1   teaspoon lime juice (optional)

Combine ingredients in a jar. Shake and refrigerate.

Mrs. Yamamoto's Cone Sushi

Makes 12

12 age triangles (see note)
8   cups water
3 ⅓ cups cooked rice
⅓   teaspoon salt
⅛   cup sugar
¼   cup cooked carrots, chopped fine
¼   cup sushi vinegar (recipe opposite)

Age Seasoning:
2 ½ cups water
½   cup soy sauce
½   cup sugar
1   tablespoon hon dashi

CRAIG T. KOJIMA

Combine the top 7 ingredients and mix gently.

Combine age in water and boil 30 minutes to remove oil; cool slightly and squeeze to remove liquid.

Combine age seasonings and bring to a boil. Add age and boil another 20 minutes. Meanwhile, combine rice with salt, sugar, carrots, and sushi vinegar.

Cool age and squeeze. Stuff with prepared rice.

Note: Age is the fried bean curd wrapper for cone sushi—or inari-zushi, in Japanese. It is sold in the Asian sections of most supermarkets in cans and packages, under various labels. Yamamoto uses a type that comes as a large square and must be cut diagonally in half, but many can be purchased already cut, sometimes in triangle and other times in rectangle shapes.

January 15, 2003

The kalbi or meat jun might be the focus of your Korean take-out plate, but everyone's got a favorite when it comes to the side dishes, too. You know what I mean, the kim chees and salads set up in the glass case. Choose four to go with your kalbi plate...

Chang Bong Choi, owner and chef at Enchanted Lake's Kim Chee Restaurant, offered his formulas for the Korean Potatoes and Cabbage Namul, two simple dishes that would add to a variety of menus—not just Korean food. I'm thinking meaty meals, such as grilled steak. The potatoes will stand up to the beefiness, and the cabbage will offer a light, refreshing counterweight.

The cabbage namul is made with just salt, pepper, and garlic. If you're used to a more pumped-up version, try a bit of hon dashi or sesame oil. Just don't overdo. A half-teaspoon may be enough.

Korean Potato

Serves 4 to 6

2	pounds potatoes, peeled, cut in bite-sized pieces
3	cups water
1	tablespoon rock salt
¼	cup soy sauce
¼	cup sugar
1	tablespoon minced garlic
½	teaspoon black pepper
1	tablespoon vegetable oil

Soak potato pieces in 2 cups of water with rock salt for 10 minutes; drain.

Combine remaining 1 cup of water with the rest of the ingredients in a shallow pan or skillet; bring to a boil and stir to dissolve sugar. Add potatoes and cook over medium-high heat, 10 to 20 minutes, stirring occasionally to coat all pieces, until tender.

Remove with a slotted spoon. If desired, drizzle 1 to 2 tablespoons of the leftover sauce from the pan over the potatoes.

Cabbage Namul

Serves 8 to 10

½	gallon water
1	head cabbage (about 3 pounds), thinly sliced
½	carrot, peeled and cut in matchsticks
½ to 1	tablespoon salt
1	teaspoon minced garlic
½	teaspoon pepper

Bring water to a boil; add cabbage and carrot. After 30 seconds, remove vegetables and rinse in cold water. Drain and toss with salt, garlic, and pepper (add salt a little at a time and taste as you go).

January 13, 1999

I don't know if I'll ever understand macaroni salad—how it came to be, why it's called a "salad," why so many people seem to need a recipe to make one. It's mayonnaise and macaroni, people!

I say this so you understand I am not a connoiseur, if there even is such a thing when it comes to mac salad. When I make it I go light on the mayo and heavy on the add-in veggies, especially watercress.

This version is based on a formula shared by Iva Kinimaka, who owns Diners in Kalihi. He works in huge quantities, carrying the formulas in his head, and there's a lot of eye-balling and "to taste" in his proportions.

When he makes mac salad, he starts with 20 pounds of noodles.

I tried reducing his recipe to make a 1-pound batch of the salad and compared it directly to a Diners' batch. The proportions didn't translate correctly, so mine turned out chunky with veggies and turned yellow from the carrots. But I like it much better than the plate-lunch standard.

If you prefer a more traditional version, double the mayonnaise and cut back on the vegetables.

The key either way is to grate the onion very, very fine. It will actually be soupy. Add the liquid and all to the salad. This allows the flavor to really blend into the noodles. It's a good trick to remember for potato salad, too.

And use Best Foods® mayonnaise. Iva insists.

Macaroni Salad

Serves 10

1   pound macaroni, cooked
1 to 2 cups Best Foods® mayonnaise
1   cup watercress, in 1/2-inch pieces
1   cup shredded carrots
¼   cup very finely grated onion
½   cup finely diced celery
¼   teaspoon salt
⅛   teaspoon pepper

Combine all ingredients, mix well and refrigerate at least one hour to allow flavors to mix and mellow.

April 21, 1999

These soy-based dishes are regular on the buffet line at the Parc Cafe—standouts even amid a sea of menu choices. Chef Robert Miller says they are among the most popular items and have been on the line for years.

The Parc Cafe, in the Waikīkī Parc Hotel, offers a number of themed buffets through the week.

Fried Tofu Salad   Serves 4 to 6

1	pound block firm tofu
¼	medium round onion, thinly sliced
2	stalks green onion, thinly sliced
1	teaspoon toasted sesame seeds
	Vegetable oil for frying

Dressing:

⅓	cup oyster sauce
1	tablespoon sesame oil
1	tablespoon soy sauce
½	teaspoon sugar
⅛	teaspoon chili pepper flakes (optional)

Cut tofu in 3/4-inch cubes, dry on paper towel, then fry in oil heated to 350°F, until light golden brown. Drain on another paper towel.

Whisk together all the dressing ingredients. Toss with tofu and add round onion slices. Garnish with green onions and sesame seeds.

Charbroiled Eggplant with Miso Dressing

Serves 4 to 6

2   round eggplants, in 1/2-inch slices
⅓   cup olive oil
     Salt and pepper to taste

Miso Dressing:
⅓   cup white miso
⅓   cup mirin
2   tablespoons rice vinegar
¼   teaspoon minced garlic
¼   teaspoon minced ginger
1   tablespoon olive oil
1   tablespoon sugar

Brush eggplant with oil and season with salt and pepper. Charbroil, or broil on top rack of oven, until golden brown and tender.

Whisk together dressing ingredients, adding a little water if too thick. Ladle dressing over eggplant; garnish with green onions if desired.

May 8, 2002

Norman Asao, executive chef at Honolulu Country Club, insists that his portobello mushrooms are nothing special. Lots of people around town marinate and broil them the same way, he says.

But having tried the mushrooms, methinks he underestimates his dish. It has become one of my favorites when I'm out to win friends and influence people. I don't even bother with the salad, I just serve up the mushrooms, sliced.

Norman usually serves the mushrooms atop a salad, or sometimes in a sandwich. And he normally uses the smaller portobellini mushrooms, about half the size of portobellos.

A couple of notes: This may seem like a lot of marinade, but I found in trying out the recipe that it does take a lot to coat the surface area of these large mushrooms, and they soak up a lot. Asao's suggestion of using a plastic bag to marinate is a good one; it's the best way to assure even coating, since the mushrooms are so bulky. Finally, try to get all the minced garlic from the marinade onto the mushrooms—during broiling, the garlic turns nice and toasty.

Portobellini Salad   Serves 4

6   portobellini mushrooms, or 2 to 3 portobello mushrooms, depending on size
8   cups mixed greens
     Grated Parmesan cheese

Marinade:
¾   cup extra virgin olive oil
6   tablespoons balsamic vinegar
2   tablespoons chopped garlic
2   teaspoons fresh thyme
     Salt and pepper to taste

Salad Dressing:
⅓   cup balsamic vinegar
⅓   cup extra virgin olive oil
⅓   cup vegetable oil
1 ⅓ tablespoons brown sugar
1   teaspoon Dijon mustard
2   teaspoons chopped garlic
     Salt and pepper to taste

Whisk marinade ingredients together. Place mushrooms and marinade in a plastic bag, seal and shake to coat mushrooms. Marinate 10 minutes.

Broil mushrooms 5 to 8 minutes per side, until cooked through. Cool, then slice.

Whisk dressing ingredients together. Toss greens with dressing, 1/4 cup at a time, to taste. Top salad with mushrooms and garnish with Parmesan cheese.

December 27, 2000

One of the world's great snack foods is edamame—soy beans. And a great, handy way to get them is frozen, already shelled, cooked and ready to eat by the handful.

I like them with just a little garlic salt. They're a really healthy treat.

But you can fancy them up, too.

Eric Leterc, executive chef at the Pacific Beach Hotel, created this salad in collaboration with Alan Wong when the two chefs opened Wong's Hawai'i Regional Cuisine Marketplace. The salad became a mainstay of the deli case.

When Leterc moved to the hotel, he gave the salad a place on his new menu.

Fresh Soy Bean Salad with Feta Cheese   Serves 2

6	ounces shelled soy beans
2	ounces diced feta cheese
1	tablespoon minced shallots
1	tablespoon diced red tomatoes
1	tablespoon diced yellow tomatoes
1	tablespoon finely sliced basil
1	teaspoon cracked coriander seed
2	tablespoons balsamic vinegar
4	tablespoons olive oil
	Pinch black sesame seeds
2	ounces grilled calamari, sliced
	Juice from half a lime
	Salt and pepper to taste

Combine all ingredients. Adjust seasonings, balancing the flavors of the lime, vinegar, and olive oil. Let sit about 20 minutes to allow flavors to blend.

The Main Event

This is where we begin. In the supermarket meat department, considering the choices: stew meat, pork chops, chicken thighs...

So many meals start here as we reach into our bag of tricks for the dishes that feed our families and get us through the week. The main dish is the marquee event. When the kids say, "What's for dinner?" They're not asking what kind of starch or vegetable you have planned.

They don't call them entrées for nothing.

Enter here.

March 24, 1999

When people tell you you've got the best spareribs on the island, you don't argue about it, even if you can't really explain why.

Tony Choi, owner of Big-Way Burger in Wahiawā, says people tell him they come from far and wide just for his spareribs. "The Kāhala post office will send someone out once in awhile."

It's a very basic recipe: Sugar, vinegar, shoyu, and ginger. What's the secret? "I don't know," Tony says. "Maybe it's the browning on the grill."

Big-Way was founded by Tony's parents, Smitty and Daisy, thirty-eight years ago. Back then they were practically alone, restaurant-wise, out in Wahiawā.

The town's complexion has changed, with fast-food outlets moving in, but Big-Way has held its own, now run by Tony and his wife, Shirley. Daisy Choi still drops by occasionally, "to see if we're doing it correctly," her son says. It was her recipes for stews, curries, ribs, and teriyaki sauce that gave the restaurant its start.

But back to the ribs. At Big-Way they're first browned on the restaurant grill. Try your frying pan, but this may be hard to duplicate at home and could well be the key to the recipe.

GEORGE F. LEE

Big-Way Burger Sweet-and-Sour Spareribs

Serves 20

10 pounds spareribs, cut in 2-inch cubes
1⅔ cups sugar
3 cups vinegar
3 cups shoyu
¾ cup crushed ginger
1½ tablespoons cornstarch

Brown meat, then transfer to a pot.

Add water to cover the meat halfway. Bring to a boil, then lower heat and cook 1 hour.

Add remaining ingredients, except cornstarch, and simmer 20 to 30 minutes. Meat should be tender but not soft enough to fall off the bone.

Mix cornstarch with water until smooth and add to ribs to thicken sauce.

Serve on a bed of cabbage with two scoops rice and kim chee.

May 26, 1999

As East meets West, kim chee diversifies. From the faithful accompanist's role in Korean cooking, kim chee slides comfortably into sandwiches and burgers. A chopped up handful in ground beef makes a mean meatloaf, in sour cream a dip that bites back.

Fried rice made with kim chee is one of the simplest dishes in the world. All the spices come with the kim chee—just add rice, and meat or an egg if you feel like it.

These recipes were developed by Toni Lee, president of the Korean Cultural Club, and Jennifer Kim, a spokeswoman for the Korean Consulate, to promote the annual Korean May Heritage Festival.

Toni uses kim chee in pizza—no tomato sauce; rather a layer of kim chee under the cheese. She hit on the idea while serving her family a Pizza Hut meal one evening. As usual, she was serving kim chee on the side.

Pizza parlors in Korea actually do offer kim chee as a topping, but Toni went after her own formula, trying various meats and flavorings. She likes pork best, especially Spam®, which is the easiest.

A final note on kim chee. It smells. If you're going to cook with it, expect the aroma to linger.

Jennifer says there is only one way to deal with that problem: "Disregard."

Kim Chee Pizza

Serves 6

1	16-inch prepared pizza crust
2	tablespoons kim chee sauce (such as Aunty Soon's brand)
2	cups won bok kim chee chopped and squeezed of all liquid
2	cups chopped Spam®
2	cups shredded mozarella cheese
	Optional toppings: Sliced bell peppers, olives, and mushrooms

Preheat oven to 425°.

Spread kim chee sauce evenly over crust. Top with kim chee, meat, and 1 cup of cheese. Add other vegetables if desired. Top with remaining cheese. Bake in 420°F oven for 10 to 15 minutes, until crust is brown.

Kim Chee Fried Rice

Serves 4

1	tablespoon vegetable oil
¼	pound pork, cut into fine shreds (may substitute diced Spam®)
2	cups chopped kim chee, rinsed and drained
	Salt and pepper to taste, optional
4	cups cooked rice (see note)

Heat oil and stir-fry pork. Add kim chee and stir-fry 3 minutes, adding salt and pepper if desired. Add rice and toss well until heated through.

Note: Rice should be prepared drier than usual; cook with less water.

January 26, 2000

The republic of nachos is a free country.

As long as you have chips on the bottom, anything goes. Top them with beef—shredded or ground—or chicken, pork, fish, or lobster, even. Add veggies (fresh or pickled), beans, salsa (any flavor), chilies, cheese (any kind, even the processed, microwave kind). Top with guacamole, sour cream, neither, or both. Create fusion mixtures as they do at Cisco's Cantina in Kailua, where co-owner Greg Blotsky makes rather inspired nachos with kālua pig and pineapple salsa.

As for the provenance of this dish—it is only loosely Mexican, the way that chop suey or fortune cookies are Chinese. That is to say, it is Mexican in style, but invented north of the border, then adopted back in the supposed homeland.

To which we say, that's very nice. We'll take some anytime.

Cisco's Nacho Grande

Serves 6

6   cups tortilla chips
6   ounces kālua pig
1   small tomato, chopped
1   small onion, chopped
½   cup chopped olives
½   cup each shredded cheddar and jack cheeses
2   tablespoons guacamole
2   tablespoons sour cream

Roasted Pineapple Salsa:
1   cup canned cubed pineapple, roughly chopped
2   tablespoons brown sugar
1   tablespoon vinegar
½   teaspoon red pepper flakes
2   tablespoon finely chopped red bell pepper
2   tablespoons roughly chopped cilantro

To make Roasted Pineapple Salsa: Combine all ingredients in a baking pan except cilantro. Broil until pineapple edges turn slightly brown, 15 to 20 minutes. Stir well; cool. Mix in cilantro. Refrigerate an hour before serving.

Preheat oven to 350°F.

On a 12-inch oven-proof serving dish, layer the nacho ingredients in the order listed, except the sour cream and guacamole. Top with pineapple salsa. Bake until cheese melts, about 5 minutes.

Top with sour cream and guacamole. Serve immediately.

December 20, 2000

When it comes to food and family, certain dishes can take on mythic proportions. A family specialty can become such a crucial part of any holiday buffet that without it, the meal can barely proceed. Often only one person in the family can really do it right.

In my extended family-by-marriage, this legendary dish is Pepsi Ham.

It tastes great and sounds cool. It's so easy that any clown can pull it off, but only one person (and her daughter) knows all the rules. As in a game of telephone, the recipe has been passed on and on, but everyone seems to remember it differently.

Use Diet Pepsi®, one person insists. Poke the ham full of holes, another says. Don't baste…baste a lot…use a 2-liter bottle…use a single can…use Coke if you want…Coke makes it bitter…

The woman who brought Pepsi® Ham into our family circle is my husband's sister's friend's mother. Her name is Sue Demola and she's from Guam, but now lives on Maui with her son, and sometimes on Oʻahu with her daughter.

Pepsi® Ham may be the easiest way in the world to guarantee a moist, juicy end product. No fussing with mustard or brown-sugar rubs, no inserting of cloves. You take a hunk of ham, pour a can or two of Pepsi® over it, cover, and bake.

Sue can't remember where she got the original recipe, but she is clear on the specifics, her daughter, Linda Cruz, says: Don't poke the ham or you'll lose juices. And do baste.

I checked the premise out with Wayne Iwaoka, professor of food science at the University of Hawaiʻi at Mānoa, who says it's the sugar in whatever soft drink you use that does the work. Exposed to roasting, it creates caramelization, adding sweetness.

Diet drinks won't work because the sweetener, aspartame, breaks down in heat. Carbonation and caramel flavoring don't make much difference.

Bottom line: A ham, precooked as it is and full of salt and/or smoke, is very hard to destroy. You could dry it out and that's about all. Pepsi® in the pan keeps that from happening, and you get to say you made a Pepsi® Ham, which is always good as a conversation starter.

Baked Pepsi® Ham   Serves 12

1   5-pound precooked ham
1   12-ounce can Pepsi®

Preheat oven to 325°F.

Place ham in a roasting pan. Pour Pepsi® over ham and seal pan with foil.

Bake, basting occasionally, 60 minutes.

Remove foil and turn ham. Baste again and bake another 30 minutes.

December 22, 2004

Pork Guisantes—better known as Filipino Pork and Peas—is one of those basic dishes that comes with just a few rules. The cook vamps from there.

Required are sliced pork, a healthy dose of frozen peas and a tomato-sauce base. Also a must: Pimientos or diced red bell peppers.

I've been doing some comparison shopping, recipe against recipe.

(Interesting aside: If you Google this dish under the alternate spelling "gisantes," the first hit is www.edcase.com, "The Official Ed Case for Congress Website." Case's wife, Audrey, maintains a collection of local-style recipes on the site—a handy tip if you're cookbook-deprived.)

Some guisantes recipes are jazzed up with fish sauce, vinegar, or even garbanzo beans. The best I found was in *The Second Plantation Village Cookbook*, published by Friends of Waipahu Cultural Garden Park. It's credited to Gloria Constantino Boylan, wife of political commentator Dan Boylan, who pronounces the dish "one of my favorites."

Gloria Boylan says she got the recipe from her uncle, Vicente Ramelb, and that it's a family favorite. In fact, she made it just last weekend.

The recipe features the intriguing addition of a half-stick of cinnamon, which does a lot to pump up the flavor. Gloria cautions not to overdo the cinnamon, though. "Once I put a little more," she said. "I thought it would make it taste better. But it didn't."

Pork Guisantes

Serves 8

2 ½ to 3	pounds pork butt, thinly sliced
4	cloves garlic
2	8-ounce cans tomato sauce
½	cup water
½	stick cinnamon, broken in small pieces
1	teaspoon salt
½	teaspoon pepper
3	bay leaves, broken in half
1	pound frozen peas
1	4-ounce bottle pimientos, thinly sliced, or 1 red bell pepper, diced

Brown pork butt with garlic. Add tomato sauce, water, cinnamon, salt, pepper, and bay leaves. Bring to a boil, then reduce heat and simmer 60 to 90 minutes.

Add peas and cook until tender. Remove pot from heat and garnish with pimiento.

September 12, 2001

It must be the moon, or something in the alignment of the stars, but the world seems to be craving pork chops, done in the Chinese, salt-and-pepper style.

Okay, not the whole world, but three people sent in independent requests, and the way I look at it, with all the foods there are to cook, a matching three-way request equals a trend.

Wilson Wu, chef and co-owner of On On Kapahulu, says these pork chops and another Chinese favorite, salt-and-pepper shrimp, are made exactly the same way. He cooks, by the way, by eyeball, with no written measurements, so this recipe is based on his approximations and my observation of the technique.

It's a simple recipe, though, so taste and make adjustments. After a few tries you should have it right.

Salt-Pepper Pork Chops or Shrimp   Serves 2

1   pound thin-sliced pork chops (about 1 pound total), cut in thirds with bone left
        on, or 12 medium shrimp, unpeeled, head-on
        Vegetable oil for frying
1   teaspoon flour
1   tablespoon minced garlic
2   large red chili peppers, sliced (about 2 tablespoons)
¼   teaspoon salt, or more to taste
½   teaspoon cooking wine
2   tablespoons chopped green onions

Fill wok with enough oil to just cover meat and heat to 350°F over medium heat.

Toss pork or shrimp with flour. Drop into hot oil and toss a couple of times. Quickly add garlic, peppers, and salt, then wine, stirring the entire time. Add green onions, toss once, then strain oil.

June 21, 2000

Howard Co opened Yen King in Kāhala Mall eighteen years ago, after a successful stint as co-owner and manager of King Tsin restaurant, where he learned to cook.

Yen King was at first devoted to the Sechuan style of Chinese cooking, but Howard is not one to hold fast to a single culinary idea. His menu now also includes foods in the Cantonese, Shanghai, Hong Kong, and Peking styles. For awhile he even served Vietnamese pho.

"Because of people's changing taste buds we are very adaptive," he says. "Whatever is selling, we keep on our menu, whatever is not selling we delete."

A straightforward philosophy. It extends to developing dishes that customers request based on foods they've tasted at mainland restaurants. Howard does this without trying the food himself. "They describe the dish to us, I call up relatives on the mainland and they go and taste, and they describe to me how it tastes."

These spareribs are a Peking-style dish.

Co boils his cooking strategy down to an acronym—HTST, for high heat, short time. He says all you need to succeed is a knowledge of how long various foods take to cook, so you know what order to throw them into the pot.

CRAIG T. KOJIMA

Spareribs in Orange Peel and Honey Sauce   Serves 4

1   pound spareribs, in 1-inch cubes, washed and drained
1   ounce piece ginger
2   stalks green onion
1   tablespoon white wine
3   quarts water
    Oil for frying and finishing
    Dash of soy sauce

Honey Syrup:
1   teaspoon vegetable oil
2   tablespoons chicken broth
2   tablespoons sugar
1   teaspoon minced orange peel
1   tablespoon soy sauce

Place spareribs, ginger, green onion, wine, and water in a pot and boil for 2 hours. Drain and cool quickly under running tap water for 5 minutes.

Heat oil to 400°F and fry spareribs 3 minutes. Drain.

To prepare Honey Syrup: Heat wok for 10 seconds; then add all ingredients. Add fried spareribs and stir vigorously for 1 minute until coated. Quickly add a dash more oil and soy sauce. Toss mixture a few times.

October 28, 1998

Lots of people consider the katsu at L&L Drive-Inn to be the gold standard in plate-lunch fare.

Eddie Flores, owner of the L&L empire, has been very generous with this recipe, sharing it not only with *Star-Bulletin* readers, but allowing me to pass it on for printing in a couple of benefit cookbooks. No doubt it lent brand-name value that helped sell a few copies for various good causes.

Eddie says chicken katsu is one of the most popular L&L dishes, right up there with barbecue chicken and short ribs.

HONOLULU STAR-BULLETIN STAFF PHOTO

Chicken Katsu   Serves 10

15 to 20   chicken thighs, about 4 pounds, boned and skinned
1   pound panko

Batter:
2   eggs
¾   cup cornstarch
¼   teaspoon each, salt, white pepper, and garlic powder
1   cup water

Katsu Sauce:
¼   cup Worcestershire sauce
½   cup ketchup
½   cup sugar
1 ¼   cups water
¼   teaspoon salt
⅛   teaspoon each chicken bouillon, white pepper, and garlic powder
            Dashes® Tabasco sauce

Preheat oil to 325°F.

Open the chicken thighs and flatten. Combine batter ingredients.

Coat chicken in batter, then in panko. Fry in oil until brown and crispy.

To make Katsu Sauce: Combine all ingredients and bring to a boil. To thicken, add a small amount of cornstarch dissolved in water. Chill.

Cut chicken into strips and serve with sauce.

March 14, 2001

Hoisin is that oh-so-Chinese sauce made of soybean paste and a host of flavorings, among them vinegar, garlic, and sugar. Its distinctive deep, sweet taste plays well off of roasted meats, and in China that's the traditional pairing.

In Hawai'i, chefs doing the fusion thing often turn to hoisin for a glaze for lamb chops, but there is a world of other possibilities.

Russell Siu of 3660 on the Rise and Kaka'ako Kitchen uses hoisin in a linguine with chicken, also incorporating chili sauce and shiso leaf.

Russell says he enjoys the sweetness that hoisin brings to a dish, but cautions that it must be used sparingly. It's a strong flavoring and too much will throw a dish off balance. He added it to the linguine, he said, to add an Asian flavor to the pasta.

FL MORRIS

Linguine with Island Chicken

Serves 4

1	tablespoon peanut oil
2	chicken breasts, boned, skinned, and sliced
1	Japanese eggplant, halved lengthwise, grilled and sliced diagonally 1/2-inch thick
8	shiitake mushrooms, stemmed and sliced
½	cup chopped oven-roasted or sun-dried tomatoes
1	tablespoon garlic, minced
¼	teaspoon crushed red pepper
2	cups heavy cream
1 ½	tablespoons soy sauce
¾	tablespoon chili sauce
¼	tablespoon hoisin sauce
¼	cup julienne shiso leaf (see note)
	Salt and pepper to taste
¾	pound dry linguine, cooked

Heat oil over medium-high heat. Brown chicken. Add eggplant, mushrooms, tomatoes, garlic, red pepper and sauté, 2 minutes. Add cream and reduce by 1/4. Add soy sauce, chili sauce, hoisin, and shiso. Season with salt and pepper. Add linguine and toss; simmer 1 minute.

Note: Shiso (sometimes spelled chiso) is a green leaf normally used to flavor ume, Japanese pickled plums. It can be found fresh in the produce section of Asian markets, normally packed in a small foam tray.

September 13, 2000

Chicken Karaage is what Chicken McNuggets® might have been, if Ronald McDonald had been Japanese.

Karaage refers to a fried, bite-sized nugget of meat and can take the form of beef, fish, pork, or chicken. A dark, gingery marinade lightly flavors the meat.

A few notes: This recipe calls for light soy sauce, which refers to the color, not to a low salt content. It is used mainly so that the chicken won't turn too dark when fried. Also to deal with that darkness problem, the temperature of the oil is lower than normal for deep-frying.

The marinade yields just enough to coat the meat, so don't expect to get so much that the meat is completely covered. You lomi the meat, or rub the sauce into the flesh.

For a variation on the dish, instead of dusting the chicken in potato starch, add the starch to the marinade and roll the chicken, marinade, and starch into little balls before frying. This is tastutaage, another traditional Japanese finger food.

Chicken Karaage   Serves 6

2   pounds boneless, skinless chicken thighs
1   cup potato starch
3   cups vegetable oil, for frying

Marinade:
2   teaspoons grated ginger
1   teaspoon minced garlic
2   teaspoons light-colored soy sauce
2   tablespoons olive oil
2   tablespoons oyster sauce
2   teaspoons lemon juice
¼   teaspoon salt
⅛   teaspoon pepper

Cut chicken into 3/4-inch cubes.

Combine marinade ingredients; taste and adjust salt and pepper. Add chicken, mixing by hand and gently massaging sauce into chicken.

Let sit about 10 minutes.

Heat oil to 325°F.

Coat each piece of chicken in potato starch. Deep-fry until lightly brown. Remove pieces with tongs or chopsticks, tapping the side of the pot to remove excess oil. Drain on paper towels. Serve with lemon slices.

December 1, 2004

Pancit is the cousin of Chinese chow mein and Japanese yaki soba—a noodle dish decorated with meat and vegetables, bound with broth or gravy.

The Filipino dish has many little brothers and sisters, among them pancit bihon, made with thin rice noodles, and pancit miki, which uses the thicker, yellow egg noodle. There's also pancit maki (with soup) and many others distinguished by type of noodle.

Pancit—like chow mein or fried rice—is customized by the cook to incorporate favorite ingredients, or whatever's at hand. This version is from Lynn Mata of Pearl City, the mother of one of my friends, which makes this a Mom Recipe, and what's better than those?

Fresh miki is easy to find in grocery stores—usually in a refrigerated section with the tofu and kim chee. Or try an Asian market.

Pancit Miki   Serves 4

4   chicken breasts or 1 whole chicken
3 to 4 cloves garlic, peeled and pounded
¼   cup vegetable oil
1   1-inch piece ginger, thinly sliced
½   large onion, coarsely diced
2   1-ounce packages dried shrimp, soaked in water 10 minutes
     Salt and pepper, to taste
½   pound fresh miki (noodles)
2   tablespoons chopped green onion, optional

Place chicken in a pot with enough water to cover. Bring to a boil, then reduce heat and simmer until cooked just enough to shred meat. Remove meat and shred into bite-sized pieces. Set broth aside.

Sauté garlic in oil, then add ginger and onion. Add chicken and shrimp. Season with salt and pepper. Simmer 5 to 10 minutes.

Add noodles (about 1/2 pound) and stir 3 minutes to mix well and heat through. Add about 2 cups of the reserved chicken broth (this amount may be adjusted, depending on how dry or soupy you like your noodles). Top with green onions.

Note: Atsuete—also called achiote or annato—may be used to add color. The seeds must be crushed in water. Add the colored water along with the broth.

October 6, 1999

Revelations that come upon us in hospital beds normally involve self-improvement and self-awareness. We vow to quit smoking, exercise more, and appreciate life and our families to a greater degree, that sort of thing.

DEAN SENSUI

June Tong's revelation was a better cookbook.

Laid up for ten days after gallstone surgery, June worked out in her mind the format for an easy-to-use recipe collection where ingredients and instructions were simplified and carefully grouped to make cooking fairly foolproof.

The result was published *Popo's Kitchen* in 1989 to mark the bicentennial of Chinese immigration to Hawai'i.

Popo's Kitchen became a standard text in local kitchens; nearly 40,000 copies were sold. Requests still come in for the book, although it's been out of print for years and June herself has diminished her public profile.

This dish, Bar-B-Que P-Nut Chicken, is one that June used to demonstrate a lot. "When I was selling my cookbook, that would really draw a crowd."

The first 5,000 copies of *Popo's Kitchen* were sold to benefit the trust fund of Darin Ihara, a teenager who had leukemia. Darin's grandparents were bowling partners of June's. Later sales benefited the American Cancer Society, Easter Seals Hawai'i, and the Chinese Bicentennial Committee. Eventually, June did sell some for herself.

A homemaker who "liked to play with

POPO'S Kitchen

THE CHINESE IN HAWAII 200 YEARS

recipes," she included her own creations and family favorites in the cookbook. She says only one case of books remains, and she's saving those, "in case I have grandchildren."

Now 68, June says she has no interest in reprinting the book. "If I print more now, then I have to go out and work again."

Bar-B-Que P-Nut Chicken

Makes about 12 sticks

5   pounds chicken boneless thighs, cut in cubes

Marinade:

1   cup soy sauce
1   cup sugar
1   tablespoon miso
1   tablespoon peanut butter
6   cloves garlic, minced
6   slices ginger, minced
2   tablespoons mirin
½   cup green onion
½   teaspoon garlic chili paste
1   tablespoon sesame oil
1   teaspoon sesame seeds

Combine marinade ingredients and marinate chicken 1 hour. Barbecue on a grill or stir-fry until cooked through. Serve pieces on sticks.

Note: June says this dish is also good without the peanut butter, for those who have peanut allergies but would like a flavorful chicken dish.

August 16, 2000

Americans have a lot of wrong ideas about Italian food, from cheesy fish to over-dressed pastas. If Fabrizzio Favale were in charge, I get the feeling he'd fix all that.

"Cheese on seafood in Italy is illegal," Fabrizzio says. "Police come and arrest you."

And that's only part of it. In a single conversation, he makes clear the firmness of his convictions. "Italian dressing, who invented that? I kill this person."

At his King Street restaurant, Mediterraneo, Fabrizzio serves the simple but true foods of his hometown, Rome. "Our menu and our recipes are straight Italian. You like, you eat. You don't like, you don't eat….I don't like compromise. A lot of people like me, a lot of people don't like me. The balance is pretty good."

True Italian food showcases quality ingredients and the best pasta, without fanciness or pretense, Fabrizzio says. "In Rome we eat very simple things, but the quality got to be good. The restaurant got to be simple."

His recipe for pomodoro sauce is indeed simple. Simple enough that he dictated the instructions as he cooked, rather than write them down. Watch him in the kitchen and he's not measuring anything anyway. Taste as you go, he says.

His purist approach keeps his restaurant busy, and it would work anywhere, Fabrizzio insists. "You invite me to your house, I open the refrigerator, I cook. Everything come good."

Pomodoro E Basilico

Serves 2

1	tablespoon olive oil
½	large onion, chopped
2	cups plain canned whole tomatoes
10	basil leaves
1	pound fresh fettucine, cooked
1	tablespoon Parmesan cheese

Heat oil; sauté onion until caramelized.

Smash tomatoes by hand, squeezing out and discarding seeds. Strain tomatoes and add liquid to the onions. Reduce slightly, then add tomatoes. Cook 10 minutes, then add basil leaves and cook another 10 minutes, covered.

Toss with pasta and cheese.

DENNIS ODA

December 9, 1998

Over at I Love Country Cafe, executive chef Dino Amorin aims to give local taste buds some international exposure.

"Locals are basically mushy eaters," Dino says. "They love their gravies, they love their stews." They also love the flavors of ginger and garlic.

And he respects all that, but won't let his training in classic French, German, and Italian cooking go to waste. The result is a large and intriguing menu featuring lots of stir-fries and stews served up with brown rice, noodles, and/or roasted vegetables. The biggest seller is lasagna.

Amorin uses no MSG and goes easy on oil, yet his dishes are high in texture and taste.

Furikake Eggplant

Serves 6

2   large round eggplants
4   tablespoons oyster sauce
     Salt and pepper to taste

Batter:
½   cup flour
1 ½ cups water
½   teaspoon salt
¼   teaspoon white pepper
2   eggs, beaten

Breading:
1   cup fine panko
1   cup furikake flakes with toasted
     sesame seeds
⅓   cup dried chopped parsley

DENNIS ODA

Peel eggplant and slice into 1/2-inch rounds. Toss with oyster sauce and sprinkle with salt and pepper. Allow to marinate in the refrigerator for 2 hours.

Mix batter ingredients together. Separately, combine breading ingredients. Dip eggplant slices in batter, then dredge in breading. Brush a frying pan lightly with a combination of canola and olive oil.

Grill eggplant over medium heat about 3 minutes per side, until coating is crisp. Eggplant will soften, but should still be firm. Serve over pasta.

Seafood

In Hawai'i it is only natural that we look to the sea for a large part of what sustains us. It's good for the heart, they say, to eat fish twice a week, and good for the soul to wander the fish market and bring home something caught fresh that morning.

Even if your seafood comes prepacked from the supermarket, though, the variety of choices and possible preparations makes a seafood meal the perfect place for exploration.

March 21, 2001

When Savas Mojarrad takes a vacation, it tends to last several years, so if you're interested in his light brand of Greek cooking, you'd best get to the Olive Tree Cafe before he decides he needs another break.

The Olive Tree, just outside of Kāhala Mall, is Savas' third Hawai'i restaurant experience. He started about thirty years ago with the Mad Greek, a night-club-restaurant on Cooke Street. Many years—and one long vacation later—came the first Olive Tree, on Ala Moana Boulevard.

He ran each for a number of years, then took six or eight years off.

"I take kind of big vacations and I say, 'I'll never do it again,'" Savas explains. "Then it takes four or five years and I forget and then I do it again."

The business simply wears a person out, he says. "You give your life away. If you want to stay out of freezers and cans, you're looking at intense work."

By that he means he avoids frozen and canned foods, as well as preservatives, additives, meat grown with hormones or antibiotics, high-cholesterol products,

GEORGE F. LEE

skin, and fat. His major avoidance: "No iceberg lettuce."

He says people will actually call and ask if he serves iceberg, as a test.

Such "intellectual eaters," are his prime targets—people who appreciate all that doesn't go into his food.

Mojarrad serves up souvlaki, or kebabs, with fish, chicken, or lamb, all skewered with onions and served with tzatziki, a yogurt sauce. For the fish version he uses fresh 'ahi, ono, mahimahi, nairagi, or other white fish.

Fresh Fish Souvlaki

Serves 4

2   pounds fresh white fish fillet
1   onion, cut in pieces ½-inch wide by 1 ½-inches long

Marinade:

¼   cup vegetable oil or light olive oil
2   tablespoons lemon juice
4   cloves garlic, crushed
1   teaspoon oregano, crushed
1   teaspoon fresh dill or ½ teaspoon dry
½   teaspoon salt
    Pinch black pepper

Remove bloodline from the fish and cut into pieces 1/2-inch thick and 1-inch square.

Combine marinade ingredients and pour over fish and onions. Refrigerate at least 2 hours. Place on bamboo skewers, alternating onion and fish pieces. Broil or grill to desired doneness.

Tzatziki (Yogurt Sauce)

4   cups plain yogurt
1   Japanese cucumber, chopped, skin on
4   cloves garlic, crushed
¼   cup fresh mint, chopped, or 1 teaspoon dry
1   tablespoon fresh dill, chopped, or 1 teaspoon dry
1   tablespoon vinegar
       Salt and pepper to taste

Line a strainer with a piece of cheesecloth and suspend over a bowl. Pour yogurt over cheesecloth. Excess liquid in the yogurt will drain into the bowl. Refrigerate overnight or until yogurt is reduced by one-third.

Combine strained yogurt with remaining ingredients and refrigerate at least 6 hours.

May 26, 1999

Catfish are the water critters of choice at 3660 on the Rise. Catfish Tempura with Ponzu Sauce was one of the original dishes created by Chef Russell Siu for his Wai'alae restaurant and remains a favorite on the menu.

"People who don't really like catfish or fishy fish, they like that dish," he said. "We have people calling in all the time to reserve catfish for the night."

The fish is farm-raised and flown in from the mainland twice a week, Russell said. The batter is light, stays crispy, and is accented by the citrus-flavored ponzu sauce.

He says the dish is quite simple. The key is a thin batter made with tempura flour and ice water, with egg yolk to produce the yellow color.

The chef suggests using an electric wok for frying because it allows for better temperature control than cooking on the stove.

A final tip: Serve the sauce UNDER the fish. Otherwise, it will make the fish soggy.

Catfish Tempura with Ponzu Sauce

Serves 4

4   8-ounce catfish fillets
     Salt and pepper to taste
½   cup flour

Tempura Batter:
1   egg yolk
4   cups water
2   cups tempura flour

Sauce:
¼   cup sugar
¼   cup sake
½   cup soy sauce
1   cup mirin
1   teaspoon grated ginger
2   tablespoons prepared ponzu sauce

DENNIS ODA

To make Sauce: combine first four ingredients in a saucepan and bring to a boil. Cool, then add ginger and ponzu.

To make Tempura Batter: Whip egg yolk into water, then slowly add mixture to tempura flour, until you have 3 cups of batter. You will not need all the water. Batter should be like a thin pancake batter and slightly lumpy. Do not overmix. Lumps will be absorbed into the batter.

Season fish with salt and pepper, then dredge in flour. Shake off excess flour and dip in tempura batter.

Heat oil to 350°F. Use enough oil so that fillets will float. Fry fish about 10 minutes, until golden and cooked through. Spoon sauce onto plate and top with fish.

December 3, 2004

A 6-foot-high, not very thick partition separates our section of the newsroom from the sports department. Occasionally an emissary from that side will cross over to talk about movies or music or, believe it or not, soap operas.

Our most frequent visitor, though, is Dave Reardon, who covers University of Hawai'i football but is also a world champion eater. He comes over a lot to talk about food, most recently to ask for a recipe for cioppino.

I was just going to hand over my cookbook until I realized that this particular recipe deserves larger exposure at this time of year—it makes for a great holiday party idea. I've used it a few times, including one Christmas Eve, and it has always drawn rave reviews, way out of proportion to its simplicity.

What you do is require each guest to bring a half-pound of shellfish. Have the broth simmering when they arrive, and add their contributions to the pot. In minutes, dinner is served, with minimal effort on your part. Add crusty bread and a salad, and the menu is complete.

Cioppino was born on San Francisco's Fisherman's Wharf, based on a northern Italian seafood stew called "ciuppin." It was a favorite of fishermen who could get a pot simmering, add whatever seafood was handy, and have a hot meal while at sea. As such, it is a dish of many variations, the only rules being that it must have tomatoes and must have seafood.

Cioppino

Serves 4

1   cup chopped onion
2   cloves garlic, minced
1   tablespoon vegetable oil
1   8-ounce can tomato sauce
1   28-ounce can tomatoes, drained and mashed
½   cup dry white wine
1   teaspoon EACH dried basil, thyme, and oregano
1   bay leaf
¼   teaspoon pepper
4   whole cloves
1 ½ pounds mixed seafood (for example, shelled shrimp, scallops, mussels, or fish
     fillets cut in 1-inch cubes)

Clam Stock:
2   tablespoons garlic
2   tablespoons olive oil
½   cup vermouth
12   clams

Sauté onion and garlic in oil until tender. Add tomato sauce, tomatoes, wine, and seasonings. Bring to a boil, then reduce heat and simmer 20 to 30 minutes.

To make Clam Stock: Sauté garlic in oil, then add vermouth and
clams. Cover and steam until clams open. Strain, reserving clams.

Add liquid to simmering cioppino pot, and allow flavors to blend,
about 4 minutes.

Stir in seafood and simmer until done. Note that fish will take longest
to cook, 3 to 4 minutes, so add that first. Shrimp should be cooked
just until it turns pink; scallops until opaque. Mussels should be
cooked just until the shells open. Add steamed clams at the end,
just before scooping up.

May 14, 2003

Douglas Tom and I have been recipe testing via e-mail, our aim being Hou See Soong, a Chinese stir-fry made with dried oysters that's served spooned onto lettuce leaves.

Douglas said he hadn't seen the dish on a menu in twenty or thirty years. I'd never heard of it, but there's nothing like a mystery.

This is apparently a dish from another generation; you won't find it in contemporary cookbooks. But I did find a few recipes in a cookbook first printed in 1941, and sent those to Douglas.

He started there, consulted friends who remember the dish, dug deep into his own memory and came up with one version. What follows is the result of both our efforts. It's not difficult or fancy, but the oysters give the dish an intriguing smoky flavor. And the lettuce-leaf wrap makes it fun to eat.

Note: Dried oysters are available in several grades. I used a medium grade that sells for $7 to $8 per half-pound bag.

Hou See Soong

Serves 4

4   ounces dried oysters
1   tablespoon vegetable oil
½   inch piece ginger, peeled and minced
½   pound ground pork
2   large dried shiitake mushrooms, soaked, finely diced
¼   cup minced bamboo shoots
¼   cup minced water chestnuts
¼   cup minced celery
¼   cup minced green onion
     Cilantro leaves, for garnish
⅛ to ¼ cup of crushed roasted peanuts (optional)
     Lettuce leaves
     Hoisin sauce, for dipping (optional)

Sauce:
1   tablespoon soy sauce
2   tablespoons sherry
2   tablespoons soaking water from oysters
1   tablespoon sugar

Soak oysters in water at least 6 hours, or overnight. Drain well, reserving 2 tablespoons of soaking water. Remove any stringy parts, then dice.

Combine sauce ingredients; set aside.

Heat oil in a large skillet or wok. Add ginger and stir-fry until fragrant. Add pork and stir-fry until no longer pink. Stir in diced oysters, then mushrooms, bamboo shoots, water chestnuts, celery, and green onion. Add sauce; stir-fry 2 minutes. Taste and adjust seasonings.

Serve on a platter, garnished with cilantro and peanuts, with lettuce on the side. Spoon mixture onto a lettuce leaf, roll up and dip in hoisin.

March 8, 2000

Never be afraid of criticism. Mike Trombetta takes it from professionals and uses it to improve the food at Harpo's.

With no formal culinary training himself, Mike invites a chef into his kitchen each year to tweak the recipes and teach better techniques to the cooks. The chef stays for three weeks to two months.

"It's nice being jostled out of your comfort zone," Mike says.

The point at Harpo's, Mike says, is to dish up the best possible Italian food, "in a casual atmosphere, at casual prices."

Case in point would be his most requested dish, the Linguine with Clams, which has become a Harpo's signature. A half portion has seven large Manila clams, a full portion is twelve, and always fresh. "A lot of people like to take a picture of a clam and pass it slowly over the linguine." Mike says he wants to load the plate with clams, "then charge what you have to charge without gouging."

Linguine with Clams

Serves 1

¼	cup diced shallots
2 ½	tablespoons minced fresh garlic
¾	cup fresh button mushrooms
4	teaspoons butter (divided use)
¼	cup dry vermouth
½	cup clam juice
⅛	cup chopped fresh parsley
1	pinch each salt, fresh ground pepper, and chopped fresh thyme
12	fresh Manila clams
¼	cup sliced green onions
⅛	cup grated parmesan cheese
12	ounces cooked linguine

Sauté shallots, garlic, and mushrooms in 3 teaspoons butter until mushrooms brown on the edges. Add vermouth and reduce all the way. Add clam juice, parsley, salt, pepper, and thyme. Bring to a boil for 15 seconds.

Reduce heat; add clams and onions and cover. Once clams open, remove them to a plate.

Add cheese and remaining teaspoon butter to the pan. Toss until butter is melted, then add pasta and toss.

Serve with clams on top of the linguine. Garnished with a parsley sprig and more green onions.

June 20, 2001

Kasuzuke is the lesser-known cousin of miso-zuke, as in Misozuke Butterfish, that well-loved, slightly sweet pairing of fish and miso.

Kasuzuke incorporates sake kasu—or sake lees, a by-product of the sake-making process. It's a light, pasty substance that resembles miso, and if it doesn't sound all that attractive, remember that miso is really fermented soy bean paste.

Sake kasu dishes are common home-style cooking in Japan, but recipes are nowhere near as easy to find as those for miso, at least not in English-language cookbooks.

So, rather than expend more time searching, I took the easy way out and asked a chef, Hiroshi Fukui of L'Uraku. It was easy for me, anyway. Turns out Hiroshi doesn't use sake kasu at his restaurant, but agreed to experiment with a batch. It was a further-pursuit-of-knowledge kind of thing.

He says kasu is frequently used in Japan with fish, especially salmon, as well as in soups and to make pickles. It is more subtle than miso and so requires more sugar and salt to bring out the flavor. That flavor is vaguely boozy, by the way—remember, the root ingredient here is sake, which is way more potent in terms of alcohol than wine. Do not serve to someone who is sensitive or allergic to alcohol.

Find sake kasu at Japanese markets, refrigerated near the miso. It's pretty cheap. You can buy it in bulk at Marukai for $5 or less for 5 pounds, but Hiroshi prefers a type that's pressed into sheets and sells for about $3 a pound at Daiei.

This recipe can be made with salmon in place of the gindara, or butterfish.

Gindara Kasuzuke

Serves 4

4   6-ounce butterfish fillets

Marinade:

6   ounces (2/3 cup) sake kasu
1   ounce (2 tablespoons) mirin
8   ounces (1 cup) water
2   teaspoons light soy sauce
¼   teaspoon white pepper
5   tablespoons sugar
2   teaspoons salt
2   teaspoons grated ginger

DENNIS ODA

Combine marinade ingredients well. Marinate fish, refrigerated, at least 18 hours.

Broil fillets 8 to 10 minutes.

October 27, 1999

Niitsuke refers to a reduced sauce of sugar and soy sauce that is served with fish. With strong-flavored

DENNIS ODA

fish such as butterfish, water is traditionally used in the sauce, but with more delicate fish such as onaga or flounder, the water may be mixed with dashi to add to the taste.

The traditional formula is 4 parts water (or water-dashi in equal amounts) to 1 part soy sauce and 1 part sugar. For those who prefer a stronger brew, the ratio can be reduced to 3–1–1.

This recipe calls for covering the fish loosely with foil, rather than a pot lid. This allows for steam to escape so the sauce reduces, without drying the fish.

My friend Cynthia, who sits two desks over, makes a version using more soy sauce (1 cup to 2/3 cup sugar and 1/2 cup water) and she uses frozen fish, without bothering to thaw it. She puts everything in a covered pot, brings it to a boil, then reduces to a simmer for 15 to 20 minutes. She also adds tofu. Her method would yield a stronger sauce without reduction (lots of water seeps out of the frozen fish). The technique you choose depends on the effect you're going for.

Butterfish Niitsuke

Serves 2

1   pound butterfish steaks
1   cup water
¼   cup sugar
¼   cup soy sauce
5 to 6   slices of ginger, 1/8-inch thick
3   stalks green onion, in 2-inch lengths

Cut fish into large chunks, leaving skin on. Place fish on the bottom of a shallow pan, in a single layer.

Combine water, sugar, soy sauce, and ginger, mixing until sugar is dissolved. Add to pot. Fish should be 3/4 covered. Cover loosely with foil.

Bring to a boil. Continue cooking rapidly about 2 minutes, until sauce begins to reduce. Remove foil and continue cooking until fish is done, another 3 minutes. As the sauce reduces, spoon liquid over the fish so it doesn't dry out. Add green onions in the last minute of cooking.

Fish will be very soft. Remove carefully. Garnish with julienned ginger and Japanese chile pepper, if desired.

Variation: Lay slices of konbu in the pot beneath the fish to add flavor and keep the fish from sticking. Gobo (burdock root) or tofu may also be added to the pot.

January 26, 2000

At $21, the bouillabaisse is the priciest item on the menu at OnJin's Cafe, and it's easy to see why, just by checking out the ingredients. You get two kinds of fish, shrimp, scallops, clams, and king crab—not to mention that precious saffron.

Chef/owner OnJin Kim says she doesn't know what it is that makes her bouillabaisse special, but it has been the highlight of more than one restaurant review.

Perhaps it's the lemongrass, or the Pernod (a licorice-flavored liqueur), or the way the fish is marinated, or the marinara sauce made specially to flavor the broth.

By the way, bouillabaisse was invented by French fishermen to make use of fish that were hard to sell, but if you want yours to be the best, use the freshest and nicest seafood you can find. The word comes from bouillir (to boil) and abaisser (to reduce).

DENNIS ODA

Bouillabaisse de Chef OnJin

Serves 6

12	1 ½-inch square pieces salmon fillet
12	1 ½-inch square pieces 'ōpakapaka or snapper fillet
12	large shrimp, shelled and deveined
8	medium scallops
6	king crab legs, cracked
6	live clams

Stock:

2	tablespoons olive oil
1	large leek, white part only, chopped
2	pieces lemongrass, white part only, diced
½	teaspoon saffron
1 ½	cups white wine
2	tablespoons lemon juice
1	quart clam juice
1 ½	cups marinara sauce (recipe follows)
½	teaspoon chopped garlic
1	tablespoon each chopped fresh basil, parsley, and cilantro
1	tablespoon Pernod

Marinade:

1	cup white wine
¼	teaspoon saffron
½	teaspoon lemon juice
½	teaspoon salt, or to taste

Continued on next page

Marinara Sauce:

2	tablespoons olive oil
½	onion, finely chopped
1	teaspoon fresh basil
½	teaspoon fresh thyme
½	teaspoon chopped fresh oregano
½	teaspoon finely chopped garlic
1	bay leaf
1	14 ½-ounce can tomatoes in juice
1	tablespoon tomato paste
¼	teaspoon each salt and pepper

To make Marinade: Bring ingredients to a boil and cook until reduced by half. Cool. Add all the seafood except the clams and marinate at least 1 hour in refrigerator.

To make Marinara Sauce: Heat oil. Add onion, basil, thyme, and oregano and sauté until onions are soft. Add garlic, bay leaf and tomatoes and simmer 30 minutes. Add tomato paste, salt, and pepper and bring to a boil 1 to 2 minutes.

To make Stock: Heat oil over medium-high heat. Add leek, lemongrass, and saffron and sauté until leek is sweaty and yellow from saffron. Add wine and lemon juice and bring to a boil. Cook until liquid is reduced by half. Add clam juice, marinara sauce, and garlic and boil again. Add basil and parsley and simmer 30 minutes. Add cilantro and Pernod and remove from heat.

To assemble dish: Bring stock to a boil. Add fish and shrimp and cook 2 minutes. Add scallops, crab, and clams and cook for 1 minute more. Divide bouillabaisse among 6 bowls. Garnish with chives and serve with toasted garlic bread.

Soups and Stews

These are the comfort dishes, the ones we turn to when we want to feel warm and satisfied. It's not surprising that so much nostalgia surrounds the memory of Grandma's oxtail soup or the beef stew Dad made every Sunday.

For the most part, these are dishes that can't rushed, and that's part of their appeal as well. It takes time to bring them to the table—they are slow-cooked so that the flavors build along with the anticipation.

April 11, 2001

Grandma's cooking is a powerful force, able to reach through the generations to yank at those taste buds.

One reader, for example, wrote of being haunted by the memory of his grandmother's dango jiru, a dumpling soup from Kumamoto prefecture in Japan.

Kengo Nozawa of Kengo's Restaurant remembers his mother serving him a version of this comfort food. "When I was small, everyday my mother would make this for me; that's all we eat."

Kengo's, being a buffet utopia, and Kengo, being used to huge quantities, the original recipe had to be broken down considerably, with translation help from Ken Saiki at the United Japanese Center.

Dango, or dumplings, take many forms in Japanese soups, from dough balls made of mochi to meatballs made with shrimp, scallop mousse, or even sardines. They may be served in soups with chicken stock, miso, konbu, or dashi as a base.

Kengo's version includes chicken and lots of vegetables. The dumplings are made with a mixture of mochiko and flour. "Comes out soft, easy to eat," he said. "That's the secret."

Kumamoto Dango Jiru   Serves 8

⅔   cup bottled tsuyu (see notes)
¼   cup prepared dashi-no-moto
5   cups water
2   pounds boneless chicken thighs, cut in 1 ½-inch pieces
1   small kabocha (see notes), peeled, cut in 1 ½-inch wedges
5   dried shiitake mushrooms, washed, soaked and halved; reserve water for stock
4   gobo tempura or vegetable tempura fishcakes, halved
5   small araimo (about 1 pound), blanched and peeled (see notes)
1   pound Chinese cabbage, cut in 1 ½-inch pieces
1   bunch watercress (about 3/4 pound), cut in 1 ½-inch pieces, for garnish

Dumplings:
½   cup flour
½   cup mochiko (sweet rice flour)
½   cup water (or less)

To make Dumplings: Combine flour and mochiko; add water slowly, stopping once a stiff dough forms. Knead thoroughly. Form small balls and flatten to silver dollar-size pieces. Drop in boiling water. Dumplings are done when they rise to the surface, about 5 minutes. Makes about 16. Set aside.

To make Soup: Bring tsuyu, dashi, and water to a boil. Add chicken; cover and cook on medium heat 10 minutes. Add kabocha, shiitake, and fishcake; reduce heat and simmer 10 minutes. Add araimo, cabbage, and dumplings; simmer another 8 to 10 minutes. Garnish with watercress.

Notes: Tsuyu is a concentrate sold in bottles for making soups and dipping sauces. Araimo, also called satoimo, is Japanese taro. Kabocha is a small, dark green pumpkin, available at most grocery stores. Find tsuyu and araimo at Asian markets.

July 20, 2005

Once upon a time, oxtails really came from oxen. Now they pretty much come from beef cattle. They really are tails, although packaged neatly in the market they don't look the part. But stand several bony segments in a line

DENNIS ODA

and pretend they're covered with skin—you could imagine a tail.

Okay, that was probably too much detail.

Oxtails are used in many cuisines, dating to times when nothing in an animal was wasted. They lend themselves to braising, and usually end up in slow-cooked soups and stews.

A Basque recipe calls for a two-hour simmer in red wine and beef stock, with carrots, onion, celery, garlic and shallots. In Italy, you might find them cooked in tomato sauce. In Vietnam, with star anise and fish sauce. Filipino kare kare adds tomatoes, peanut butter, and annatto.

The version we consider "local" is usually an Asian-style mix with ginger, star anise, and sometimes whiskey. Peanuts are normally required as well. While pasta is a common accompaniment in Italy and rice noodles in Vietnam, around here it's plain white rice.

This version comes from the Prince Golf Club's Bird of Paradise restaurant.

The important thing to remember about oxtails is to skim the broth often during cooking. This reduces the greasiness and residue.

Oxtail Soup
Serves 10

5 to 6 pounds oxtails
1 15-ounce can chicken broth
1 15-ounce can beef broth
3 pieces star anise
2 bay leaves
1 teaspoon pepper
1 3-inch piece ginger, smashed
5 cloves garlic, minced
1 pound shelled, unsalted peanuts

Suggested condiments:
Grated ginger
Blanched choi sum
Cilantro sprigs

Place oxtails in a large pot and cover with water. Bring to a boil. Strain and rinse.

Return oxtails to pot. Add chicken and beef broths, plus enough water to cover oxtails. Bring to a boil, then reduce heat. Add star anise, bay leaves, pepper, ginger, and garlic. Simmer 2-1/2 to 3 hours, until oxtails are tender. Skim fat throughout the cooking process.

In the last half hour, add peanuts. Serve with condiments.

April 30, 2003

The Paniolo Beef Stew served at the Hale Koa Hotel is Hawaiian in name, but not in flavor. Think of it as paniolo equals cowboy equals southwestern.

Rolf Walter, the hotel's executive chef, said the dish is basically a beef stew with peppers, in a Tex-Mex style.

I've adapted the recipe from an original that serves 50. It makes a flavorful pot of stew that owes a great deal of its distinctive taste to Dijon mustard.

Paniolo Beef Stew

Serves 12

¼	cup vegetable oil
5	pounds stew meat, cubed
½	cup flour
1	large onion, sliced thin
3	large tomatoes, seeded, in 1/2-inch dice
2	ounces serrano chilies, seeded and diced (use gloves when handling)
3	large cloves garlic, minced
¼	cup packed brown sugar
1	12-ounce can beer
2	cups water
¾	cup Dijon mustard
½	teaspoon ground cumin
1	teaspoon oregano
¾	teaspoon allspice
½	teaspoon cayenne pepper
½	teaspoon salt, or to taste
1	green bell pepper, julienned
1	red bell pepper, julienned
1	cup frozen corn kernels, defrosted and drained
	Cilantro leaves, for garnish

Heat 1 tablespoon of the oil in a large skillet. Pat beef cubes dry and dredge in flour, shaking off excess. Brown meat on all sides, working in batches; add more oil with each batch. Place in a large pot.

Sauté onions in the same skillet until soft. Add tomatoes, chilies, garlic, and brown sugar. Add beer and deglaze—scraping bottom of pan to loosen any browned bits. Add mixture to meat in pot.

Add water, mustard, and spices to pot and bring to a boil, stirring often. Reduce heat and simmer about 1-1/2 hours, until meat is tender. Skim fat.

Add bell peppers and corn; cook 5 minutes more. Garnish with cilantro.

Note: The recipe calls for 2 ounces of serrano chilies, seeded, which tames a lot of the heat. The Hale Koa original called for a lot more than I used, but I'll leave the exact amount up to you. My supermarket serranos were still pretty frisky after seeding, so adjust the amount based on the freshness of your peppers and your own tolerance, not to mention how much time you want to devote to the laborious task of seeding (be sure to use gloves when handling the peppers).

February 10, 1999

Many people swear by the mango chutney, but for legions of others it's the Portuguese Bean Soup that marks the Punahou Carnival with good taste.

Thankfully, the school is willing to share.

Jimmy Hashimoto, father of three Punahou graduates, is master of the bean soup, which is prepared in gigantic proportions during the annual carnival.

He and his bean-soup volunteers cook up 1,800 gallons a year.

It's especially filling, with cabbage and macaroni cooked in.

To cut the fat in this soup, try a technique recommended in other similar recipes: Cook the ham hocks a day ahead and refrigerate the broth. The next day, remove the hardened layer of fat atop the broth, then complete the soup.

DENNIS ODA

Punahou Portuguese Bean Soup
Makes 10 large servings

1   pound ham hocks
3   small cans kidney beans
2   large potatoes, cubed
3   large carrots, diced
1   medium onion, chopped
1   cup celery, chopped
1   16-ounce can crushed tomatoes
1   16-ounce can tomato sauce
1   pound Portuguese sausage, diced or cubed
1   cup macaroni, uncooked
1   teaspoon granulated garlic
1   tablespoon sugar
    Salt and pepper to taste
1   medium head of cabbage, cubed

Boil ham hocks in 2 quarts water until tender (save stock). Cut meat from the bones.

Bring ham stock to a boil and add the cut meat and all the remaining ingredients except the cabbage. Simmer for 1 hour, stirring frequently. If too thick, add a little water. Add the cabbage, cook until tender.

December 19, 2001

Given all the stresses of hanging out at a hospital, a dish spooned up in the cafeteria is not what you'd normally think of as comfort food. But the beef stew served at the Queen's Hospital cafeteria does seem to work for hospital visitors.

Vivian Coppock, director of food services at Queen's Medical Center, said the stew is on the menu daily and is very popular.

"It's a favorite," she said. "People in Hawai'i really like beef stew."

Vivian is a 20-year veteran of food service in health systems, but she's been in Hawai'i just two years, having moved here from Oklahoma.

She provides an interesting perspective on stew, which we tend to think of as a universal dish. The Queen's version, she says, is very different from what she's seen served on the mainland. The beef is cut smaller here, for one thing, and potatoes don't play as big a role (got rice; that's why).

Also, the peas. Vivian says she isn't used to seeing tiny little peas in a big, hearty stew.

That said, here's the recipe. Nothing fancy, but if it can provide solace to people visiting hospitalized friends and relatives, it must be comfort food indeed.

Queen's Hospital Beef Stew

Serves 8

1	teaspoon vegetable oil
2	pounds beef, cut in 1-inch square pieces
1 ½	cups diced onion
1	teaspoon salt
1	teaspoon pepper
2	beef bouillon cubes
1 ½	cups water
2	bay leaves
½	cup tomato paste
½	cup canned, diced tomatoes
1	teaspoon chili pepper sauce
2	cups diced celery
1 ½	cups diced carrot
2 ⅛	cups diced potato
2	tablespoons cornstarch, dissolved in 1/4 cup cold water
¼	cup frozen peas

Heat oil in skillet. Brown meat over medium heat. Add onions and cook until onions are transparent. Add salt, pepper, beef bouillon cubes, water, bay leaves, tomato paste, diced tomatoes, and pepper sauce.

Bring to a boil, then reduce heat to low and simmer until meat is tender. Add more water if necessary. Add celery, carrots and potatoes and simmer until vegetables are tender.

Add cornstarch mixture to stew. Simmer a few minutes. Add peas and simmer 4 minutes.

March 3, 2004

The Aloha Aina Cafe sits across Farrington Highway from the Wai'anae McDonald's. It's an interesting juxtaposition: Aloha Aina's plantation-era, soothing green, all-wood decor vs. McDonald's plasticine ambiance. Alona Aina's organic greens vs. McDonald's french fries.

RONEN ZILBERMAN

It's as though the anti-McDonald's had set up shop on the steps of a shrine to fast food.

"We're kinda the odd corner out," says Kukui Maunakea-Forth, who helps run the cafe. It's not just McDonald's that makes up their neighborhood; there's a KFC down the street and all manner of modern quick-eat joints nearby.

It seems that Aloha Aina was born to be different.

The cafe is an offshoot of Mala 'Ai 'Opio, an organic farm in Wai'anae that goes by its nickname, MA'O Organic, an internship program for low-income youths. Training goes beyond planting and harvesting, however. Marketing is key to success, so the participants are expected to become proficient in that area as well. Thus, they sell their produce at mini-farmers' markets and volunteer at the cafe.

The menu is homespun and simple: banana pancakes, chili, quesadillas, salads made with the farm's organic greens, a killer pumpkin crunch dessert.

Chisa Dodge, the cafe's cook, shared her recipe for chili, which has come to be the one I make for my kids at home. Hardly more complicated than a package mix, but much better.

Aloha Aina Cafe Turkey Chili   Serves 6 to 8

1	pound ground turkey
1 ½ to 2	cups chopped yellow onion
1	tablespoon vegetable oil
4	cloves garlic, minced, or 1 teaspoon garlic powder
1	tablespoon fresh chopped oregano
1	tablespoon cumin powder
1	cup canned pinto beans
1	cup canned black beans
1 ½	cups tomatoes sauce
2	tablespoons chili powder, or to taste

Brown turkey and onion in vegetable oil. Add garlic, oregano, and cumin; sauté. Add beans, tomato sauce, and chili powder. Bring to a boil, then reduce heat and simmer 20 minutes.

RONEN ZILBERMAN

Breads

Does the idea of a low-carb diet make you want to flee? Do you need your bread? This collection is for you.

These breads are life's extras. You don't need them to survive—you can get your grains and essential carbohydrates from brown rice and pasta, after all— but they certainly make life more interesting, more grounded—more... filling.

September 8, 2004

The ensemada has absolutely no nutritional value, unless you consider happiness to be good for the health. Light, buttery, and full of sugar, it is the ultimate empty carb. But you only live once, right?

For those unfamiliar with this fabulous pastry, an ensemada—sometimes spelled ensamada or ensaimada—has Spanish origins, but is best known in Hawai'i in its Filipino version, a large, coiled bun spread with a butter and sugar topping.

In Majorca, Spain, where these buns are a breakfast basic, they may be topped with pumpkin custard or with bits of squash or sausage. Some Filipino recipes have them filled with cheese.

This version is more like the type sold in our local bakeries.

It may be a bit complicated for a beginner, but it's not hard to get excellent results the first time. Note that the dough is very, very soft. Do not be alarmed. This gives you a nice, airy end product.

Also, note that this recipe makes 12 large buns. If you can't consume them all at once, spread only a few with butter and sugar for immediate eating. Warm the leftovers up in a toaster oven and top them off at that time.

Or, omit the topping and these make very nice dinner rolls.

Ensemada

Makes 12 rolls

½	cup evaporated milk
½	cup water
½	cup sugar
½	cup butter
4	cups sifted flour
6	egg yolks, slightly beaten
2	packets (2 tablespoons) yeast plus 1 tablespoon sugar, dissolved in 1/2 cup warm water

Topping:

¼	cup softened butter
	Sugar, for dusting

Combine milk and water. Heat on stovetop until just below boiling. Add sugar and butter; stir to melt butter. Place in large mixing bowl and let cool.

Gradually mix in flour and egg yolks, then yeast/sugar mixture. Mix well. Dough will be soft and sticky. Form into a ball and place in clean, greased bowl. Cover and let rise 30 to 45 minutes, until double in bulk.

Cover 2 large baking sheets with parchment.

Spread butter on work surface. Rub some butter on hands to prevent sticking. Divide dough into 2 parts. Throw dough onto work surface about 10 times to firm it up.

Divide each portion of dough into 6 balls. Form each ball into a rope, rolling and stretching until about 12 inches long. Coil each rope onto cooking sheet, making a snail-shell shape. Leave 2 to 3 inches between rolls. Let rise 40 minutes.

Preheat oven to 350°F.

Bake buns 10 to 15 minutes, until light brown.

Cool slightly, then spread with butter and dust with sugar.

October 1, 2003

There is something magical about the blueberry scones baked at Diamond Head Market and Grill in Kapahulu. Visit the market at 7:30 a.m., and you'll find people lined up for these scones—full of whole berries and chunks of cream cheese.

The establishment's top exec, Kelvin Ro, former owner of the Kāhala Moon, has always been generous in sharing his recipes, but in this case he declined. He's selling more than 200 a day, Ro says, and his pastry chef would rather keep the recipe in-house.

But it seemed worthwhile to take a stab at the recipe. I studied a number of recipes for cream-cheese scones and biscuits and came up with this. Is it the same? Absolutely not. Is it good? You betcha.

By the way, the difference between a biscuit and a scone? Milk (or cream), sugar, and eggs—found in scones and not in biscuits. Also, biscuits are normally cut in circles or just dropped onto cookie sheets, while scones are rolled out and cut into triangles.

The Diamond Head scones taste of cream, sugar, and egg, but they are dropped, not triangulated, so consider them a hybrid. They also have a sugary glaze, but I don't think it's necessary with this recipe.

Blueberry Cream Cheese Scones

Makes 8 scones

⅓ cup butter, cut in pieces

2 cups flour

½ cup sugar

2 teaspoons baking powder

¼ teaspoon salt

⅓ cup milk

3 ounces cream cheese, softened

1 egg, beaten

½ cup frozen blueberries, thawed, rinsed, and drained, sprinkled with sugar

2 ounces cream cheese, cut in 1/2-inch pieces

Preheat oven to 400°F.

Combine butter, flour, sugar, baking powder, and salt in a bowl and cut with a pastry blender or two butter knives until crumbly. Stir milk into softened cream cheese, then stir in egg until well combined. Stir cream cheese mixture into flour mixture until dough forms a ball.

Gently fold blueberries and cream cheese pieces into the dough to incorporate evenly. Be careful not to crush the berries or mash the cream cheese pieces.

Spoon mounds of dough onto an ungreased cookie sheet to make 8 scones. Tuck berries and cream cheese pieces into the dough as much as possible. (Or, for traditional scones, gently pat the dough into a 9-inch circle on the cookie sheet. Sprinkle with sugar. Cut into 8 wedges, but do not separate.)

Bake for 18 to 20 minutes, until golden.

September 6, 2000

Want to make everyone in the office love you? Bake. Works every time. Put out a plate of these babies at break time and everyone will think you're a genius.

The recipe is from Heidi's Bistro and Delis, owned by Micki Mortensen.

The pineapple is Mortensen's personal favorite, but she says all her muffins are a point of pride.

"The muffins are as old as we are," she says. "I remember in '74 or '75 when we decided to make the best muffins in town."

She and a baking friend took to the kitchen and tested batch after batch.

The original recipe makes 8 dozen, so this one has been broken down to make a manageable dozen. Don't expect them to turn out exactly the same, but they should be close.

Heidi's Pineapple or Blueberry Muffins

Makes 1 dozen

2   eggs
1 ½   cups sugar
½   cup plus 1 tablespoon water
¾   cup margarine
3 ⅓   cups flour
¾   cup powdered milk
2 ¼   teaspoons baking powder
¼   teaspoon salt
¾   cup drained, crushed pineapple, or frozen blueberries, defrosted

Preheat oven to 350°F. Line a muffin pan with baking cups.

Place ingredients in a mixer in the order listed, except fruit. Mix 2 minutes at low speed, then for 30 seconds at fast speed. Add fruit. mix 30 seconds at slow speed.

Pour batter into muffin pan. Bake 1 hour or until golden, turning the pan every 15 minutes. Makes 1 dozen.

September 11, 2002

Sandy Kodama is known as "Mom," not just to her six children, but also to the staff and many of the customers at Sansei Seafood Restaurant & Sushi Bar.

Her son, D. K., owns the place, and she's his secret weapon.

She greets customers, serves tables, pours water, helps train the kitchen staff, and cooks, too. Most important to the guys in the *Star-Bulletin* newsroom, she usually bakes oatmeal cake on Fridays. It's a dense, flavorful cake, but what the guys like is the topping—a hearty, heavy mixture of coconut, walnuts, and macadamia nuts.

This recipe's for them.

CRAIG T. KOJIMA

Sansei Oatmeal Cake
Serves 12

1 ½   cups boiling water
1   cup oatmeal (not instant)
1   cup white sugar
1   cup brown sugar
2   eggs, well beaten
½   cup butter
1 ⅓   cups flour
1   teaspoon cinnamon
1   teaspoon baking soda
1   teaspoon salt

Topping:
6   tablespoons butter
¼   cup evaporated milk
½   cup brown sugar
½   teaspoon vanilla
1   cup shredded coconut
1   cup chopped walnuts
1   cup chopped macadamia nuts (optional)

Preheat oven to 350°F. Grease a 9 x 13-inch pan.

Pour water over oatmeal and let stand 20 minutes. Add sugars, eggs, and butter to oatmeal.

Combine flour, cinnamon, baking soda, and salt. Stir into oatmeal mixture. Pour into prepared pan. Bake 30 minutes.

Combine topping ingredients and spread over baked cake. Place under broiler until bubbly and golden.

February 26, 2003

The soft pretzel, staple food of ball games and shopping excursions to the mall, is a good entry-level item for bakers just entering the world of yeast. The formula that follows is pretty much idiot-proof.

The pretzels are crunchy on the outside; soft on the inside and taste like the real deal, especially hot out of the oven.

Although the ingredients and the procedure are fairly simple, this is not fast food. It takes more than an hour for the dough to rise, in two different steps. Then you form the pretzels, boil them, bake them, and THEN you eat them. It's the boiling that defines the texture.

One note for beginners: Be careful of the water temperature when dissolving the yeast—use a thermometer. Too hot, you'll kill the yeast; too cool, it won't work at all.

Now, as for presentation, you can form your dough into a pretzel shape, but that takes practice. I just made sticks. It all tastes the same.

Soft Pretzels

Makes 12 large pretzels or 24 sticks

1   packet active dry yeast (scant tablespoon)
1   cup warm water (115°F to 120°F—NOT boiling)
2 ¾ cups flour
1   tablespoon sugar
½   teaspoon salt
2   tablespoons vegetable oil or softened butter
4   cups water
2   tablespoons baking soda
2   tablespoons coarse salt

Add yeast to warm water; let sit 5 minutes.

Combine 1-1/2 cups flour, sugar, salt, and oil in a large mixing bowl. Add yeast mixture and stir until well-combined. Add remaining 1-1/4 cups flour. Knead dough 3 minutes; form into a ball. Let sit 1 hour. Dough should double in size.

Divide dough into 12 pieces and roll each piece into a ball (dust hands with flour to prevent sticking). Place balls on a cookie sheet or lightly floured surface. Let rest 15 minutes.

Roll each ball into a 16-inch length and form into a pretzel shapes. Or, divide each ball in half and roll each half into a 3-inch stick, about 3/4-inch wide. Let rest a few minutes.

Preheat oven to 475°F. Grease a large cookie sheet. In a non-aluminum pot, bring remaining 4 cups water to a boil; stir in baking soda.

Add pretzels to the boiling water in batches (do not crowd pot) and boil 1 minute, turning once. Shake off excess water. Place pretzels on cookie sheet and sprinkle with coarse salt. Bake 10 minutes, until golden brown. Best eaten right out of the oven.

March 31, 1999

Part 1 of this story: In Kona a generation ago, Mona Kahele learned to make Peanut Butter Bread from her grandmother. They even made their own peanut butter from peanuts grown on their farm in the days before everyone planted coffee. In 1982, she donated the recipe to *The Kahikolu Country Cookbook*, published by Kahikolu Congregational Church.

Part 2, nearly 20 years later: A woman in Florida e-mailed in search of a Peanut Butter Bread recipe. She'd had one—in a World War II cookbook—but it was lost. It was an economical wartime recipe that didn't use butter, she said, and her family loved it.

The Florida woman's request was published in the *Star-Bulletin*, prompting a reader to reach way back in her brain and bookshelf. She came up with the Kahikolu Church cookbook. A call to the church turned up Mona, living in a retirement home in Captain Cook.

Mona remembers adapting her grandmother's recipe, adding more peanut butter, to satisfy her daughter's taste buds.

That daughter was among 23 children—two adopted and the rest hānai—raised by Mona and her fisherman husband.

She said she learned to cook in the home of her Portuguese grandmother on her father's side. "Everything is bread, bread, bread."

If you love peanut butter, this bread is quick, easy, and cheap. And it's particularly good fresh out of the oven, when it's reminiscent of peanut butter cookies.

Peanut Butter Bread

Makes 1 loaf

2 cups flour
4 teaspoons baking powder
1 teaspoon salt
¼ cup sugar
⅔ cup peanut butter
1 ¼ cups milk

Preheat oven to 350°F. Grease loaf pan.

Combine dry ingredients. Add milk to peanut butter; combine well.
Add peanut butter to flour; mix well. Pour into pan and bake 45 to 50
minutes.

GEORGE F. LEE

Sweet Thoughts

When it comes to a potluck, everyone wants to bring dessert. This is partly because dessert is easy—you can always stop at Zippy's after work and buy a pie. But it's also because dessert is show-off time. Desserts are attention-getters—pretty, sweet and often spectacular.

But when you think about it, desserts have to work hard. People are full, everyone's on a diet. You have to be really good to claim your share of stomach space.

Bottom line: Don't ignore this part of the meal. When it comes to dessert, it's show time.

October 17, 2001

It has come to my attention that there are people who cannot eat chocolate. They have allergies, or find that chocolate triggers migraines, or they have to avoid the milk or the caffeine found in chocolate.

The world can certainly be a cruel place.

But at least the world does provide carob, a substitute for chocolate that's higher in natural sugar, lower in fat, and minus the caffeine. Some people actually prefer it to chocolate.

Down to Earth Natural Foods offered this carob chip cookie recipe, which is used in the store's cooking classes.

General baking cookbooks tend to ignore this substance. In index after index, between cardamom and carrot, you'll find a whole lot of nothing. But vegetarian cookbooks do pay the ingredient heed. It's favored by vegans because carob powders and some carob chips are made without milk products.

Carob comes from the dried pulp of the carob or locust bean and is sold at health food stores. But before you toss a handful of carob chips into your mouth, hear this: The taste is very pungent, and not really like chocolate. Some people love it, but others can't handle it at all.

Carob Chip Cookies

Makes about 3 dozen cookies

1   cup butter, softened
1   cup packed raw sugar
2-½ cups flour
½   teaspoon baking soda
¼   teaspoon sea salt
½   cup fructose (see notes)
1   tablespoon powdered egg
        replacer with 4 tablespoons
        water (see notes)
2   teaspoons vanilla
2   cups carob chips

RICHARD WALKER

Preheat oven to 300°F.

Cream butter with sugar, then mix in all other ingredients, adding the chips last. Drop by tablespoons onto a greased cookie sheet. Bake 18 to 22 minutes.

Notes: Fructose and powdered egg replacer are sold at health food stores. Fructose may also be found near the sugar in supermarkets. Substitute 2 eggs for the egg replacer in this recipe.

May 28, 2003

Did you know that if you leave a bag of chocolate chips in a hot car for an hour at high noon they don't even begin to melt? Tried it this weekend, not on purpose, so it was a relief.

Thus it was possible to test recipes made with chocolate chips and cornflakes.

This one is fairly basic, with the cornflakes providing a bit of crunch. It could handle more cornflakes or more chocolate chips, depending on whether you'd like to vary either of those taste sensations.

Cornflake Cookies with Chocolate Chips   Makes about 48 cookies

1   cup (2 blocks) butter
1   cup sugar
2   eggs
1   teaspoon vanilla
2   cups flour
1   teaspoon baking soda
1   cup crushed cornflakes
1   cup semisweet chocolate chips (more if you like)
1   cup chopped nuts, optional

Preheat oven to 300°F.

Cream butter and sugar. Beat in eggs, 1 at a time. Stir in vanilla. Add flour and baking soda; mix well. Fold in cornflakes, chocolate chips, and nuts. Drop by teaspoonfuls on ungreased cookie sheet. Bake 15 minutes.

August 27, 2003

This request was so odd it was fascinating. A reader wrote in for a recipe for cookies made with okara, or soy bean meal. Okara is a leftover product of tofu-making, mealy and sawdust-like. It has lots of nutritional value—protein, calcium, and fiber—and because it's cheap, okara is used in a number of traditional Japanese dishes and as a filler in meat patties.

Baking with okara is relatively new territory, but not entirely uncharted.

The okara works as a substitute for part of the flour. It seems to mellow the whole wheat flour, making cookies that are quite soft and chewy.

This cookie is moist and fruity, like an oat cake, similar to those so popular in coffee bars.

You'll need plain okara, sold in bags at Japanese markets such as Daiei. Another version of okara is sold in tubs and includes bits of vegetables and seasonings.

Okara Oatmeal Cookies   Makes about 2 dozen cookies

¼   cup oil
½   cup honey
¼   cup lightly packed brown sugar
½   teaspoon vanilla
1   cup okara
½   cup whole wheat flour
1 ½   cups rolled oats
½   teaspoon baking soda
½   cup dried fruits (raisins, cranberries, chopped dates, etc.)
¼   cup sunflower seeds
¼   cup milk

Preheat oven to 350°F.

Combine oil, honey, sugar, and vanilla. Stir in okara, flour, oats, and baking soda. Mixture will be dry. Use hands to fold in fruit and sunflower seeds. Moisten with milk, a little at a time. Dough will be crumbly, but should hold together when formed into a ball.

Roll balls of dough 2 inches across and place on a greased cookie sheet. Flatten to 1/2-inch thickness. Bake 12 to 15 minutes, until light brown.

Variation: Carob or chocolate chips may be substituted for some or all of the dried fruit.

May 19, 2004

I met someone interesting on the Internet last week—Pat Dwigans of Greenwood, Ind., also called Cobra Mom, who runs something called OPMALE STAR.

Dwigans coordinates pen pals and care packages for U.S. troops abroad (full name Operation Make a Life Enriched Saying Thanks and Remembering; OPMALE STAR being much easier to articulate). But before taking on that duty, she managed the Web site www.busy-cooks.com.

Dwigans' footprints are all over the Internet, attached to a variety of recipes that have no doubt been picked up and spread around by other cooks.

I found her while researching a recipe request for a tofu-walnut bar. There are a number of Internet postings for tofu cookies, but all the recipes were the same and all led back to Dwigans.

Dwigans is pretty much consumed by the group she founded in 1995 and doesn't do much recipe posting anymore, although she's still an avid cook. "I love cooking and love trying new recipes."

I've adjusted it a bit to turn it from a drop cookie to a bar. This is an adult treat (my daughter pronounced it "boring") that would go nicely with a cup of coffee or tea. It's rather dense, not too sweet, and a bit spicy with all the ginger.

Don't look at it as a health bar, despite the tofu—it's made with honey and a half cup of butter. The tofu seems to add moisture and a bit of protein. The recipe could be modified to add more nuts or perhaps even chocolate chips.

Tofu-Walnut Cookie Bar   Makes about 2 dozen bars

1 ½   cups whole-wheat flour
½   teaspoon baking soda
½   teaspoon salt
1   cup dried fruit (raisins, dried cranberries, chopped dates or
        prunes, or a combination)
½   cup chopped walnuts
1   teaspoon ginger
1   teaspoon cinnamon
1   teaspoon nutmeg
½   cup honey
½   pound soft tofu, well-drained
1   egg
½   cup butter, softened
1   teaspoon vanilla

Preheat oven to 350°F. Grease a 9 x 13-inch pan.

Combine flour, baking soda, salt, fruit, nuts, and spices.

Put honey, tofu, and egg in a blender. Blend until smooth. Combine
with butter and vanilla.

Fold wet ingredients into dry and stir to moisten. Press into baking
pan. Bake 20 minutes.

Cool and cut into squares.

May 19, 2001

Susy Kawamoto is the best cookie baker I know and often comes up with solutions to recipe mysteries. In this case, she granted a reader's request for a cookie made with arare.

It is quite good, especially right out of the oven. I ate five before I remembered my diet.

A couple of notes: This seems like a lot of butter, and the dough is quite greasy, but it's right. Also, you can crush the arare very fine or go for more of a coarse crush. I'd go for a fine crush if you expect to keep the cookies around for several days. Larger chunks of arare tend to get too chewy and stick to the teeth (you know how arare gets after just a little time in humid air).

Susy also offered a recipe for mochiko cookies, a good match in taste and texture for the popular Keith's mochiko shortbread, although they don't bake up into the same familiar little mounds.

Kawamoto says you can experiment with mochiko—Japanese rice flour—in adapting your own favorite recipes. Substitute mochiko for a portion of the flour in the recipe, but never more than 1 cup mochiko to 1 cup of flour.

Arare Cookies

1 ½   cups butter, softened
1   cup firmly packed brown sugar
1 ½   teaspoons baking soda
2   teaspoons vanilla extract
1   tablespoon soy sauce
1   egg
3   cups flour
1 ¾   cups Rice Krispies®
1-½   cups mochi crunch, crushed (Tomoe
      brand recommended)

Preheat oven to 350°F.

Cream softened butter and brown
sugar until light and fluffy. Add   F.L. MORRIS
baking soda, vanilla, soy sauce,
and egg and beat well. Add flour and mix until just well-blended. Add
Rice Krispies® and crushed mochi crunch and mix well.

Roll into 1-inch balls and place 2 inches apart on cookie sheet; flatten
slightly. Bake 8 to 10 minutes or until golden.

Mochiko Butter Cookies

½	pound butter, softened
¾	cup sugar
1	teaspoon baking soda
2	teaspoons vanilla
1 ½	cups flour
½	cup mochiko
1	cup chopped macadamia nuts (optional)

Preheat oven to 350°F.

Cream butter and sugar until light and fluffy, 5 to 8 minutes. Add baking soda and vanilla. Mix well. Add flour, mochiko, and chopped nuts, if using; blend well. Drop by rounded teaspoonfuls onto cookie sheet and bake 15 to 20 minutes or until slightly golden.

February 20, 2002

Mamon, a Filipino sponge cake, is a good choice if you're baking a cake from scratch for the first time.

Once you get a hold of the cake flour and separate the six eggs, you'll find it's not much harder than a Pillsbury mix. Plus you can compare your results to a professional mamon—say, from Golden Coin.

Mamon   Makes 24 cupcakes

1   cup cake flour
1   teaspoon baking powder
6   eggs, separated
1   teaspoon cream of tartar
1   cup sugar
1   teaspoon vanilla
½   cup vegetable oil

Preheat oven to 350°F. Grease muffin cups, or line with paper baking cups.

Sift together cake flour and baking powder; set aside.

Beat egg whites and cream of tartar until very foamy, but not stiff. While continuing to beat add: sugar, gradually, then vanilla and oil, then egg yolks, one at a time, then the flour and baking powder.

Fill muffin cups with batter, about 2/3 full. Bake 12 to 15 minutes or until a pick inserted in the center of a cake comes out clean.

April 14, 2002

This cake goes by many names—Mushi Cake, Steamed Cheesecake, Soufflé Cheesecake, Golden Cheesecake.

Whatever the label, it is the Japanese version of Western cheesecake. You'll find it sold in snack-size portions in Japanese markets, packaged in plastic like Twinkies®—it's even the same golden color as Twinkies®, but not at all similar in taste.

The Japanese import is less cheesy and more cakey than a standard cheesecake. There's really no comparison among Western pastries, so it's hard to explain. But if you try one, you'll likely be hooked.

A few recipes turned up on Japanese Web sites. Although written in English, much was lost in translation, so I went through three test batches. Two went straight into the trash.

In the end it turned out to be a fairly simple project. Mix up some cream cheese and milk with cornstarch (not flour). Separately whip up a meringue of egg whites and sugar. Combine and bake in a bain-marie, or water bath, which simply is a pan filled with water. One tip here: Most electric ovens vent through the back right burner on the stovetop. Be sure nothing is covering that burner when you're baking with a water bath, or you'll end up with a sopping stovetop.

The cake will rise considerably in the oven, then sink as the cake cools, to form a nicely textured, dense dessert. In Japan, this type of cake is often served with melted jam on top as a glaze.

Japanese Cheesecake

Makes one 9-inch cake

7   ounces cream cheese at room temperature
¼   cup whole milk
¼   cup ultra fine sugar (sometimes called caster sugar)
3   egg yolks
¼   cup cornstarch
2   tablespoons lemon juice
2-½ cups boiling water

Meringue:
3   egg whites
¼   cup ultra fine sugar
½   teaspoon cream of tartar

Preheat oven to 350°F. Spray a 9-inch cake tin (round or square) with cooking oil spray.

Beat cream cheese with milk to soften. Add sugar, egg yolks, cornstarch, and lemon juice. Beat until smooth.

To make Meringue: Beat egg whites in a separate bowl until foamy. Gradually add sugar and cream of tartar, beating on high speed until soft peaks form, about 8 minutes. (If your kitchen is unusually warm or humid, it helps to chill the beaters and bowl. And always make sure both are completely clean and dry.)

Gradually fold beaten meringue into cream-cheese mixture, stirring gently until thoroughly combined. Pour into cake pan and smooth surface. Place cake pan into a larger roasting pan and place on lower rack of oven. Pour enough boiling water into roasting pan to come half-way up the side of the cake pan. Bake 35 to 40 minutes, until a pick inserted into the center comes out clean.

Cool in the pan on a rack, then unmold cheesecake.

December 11, 2002

Debbie Puente was born to meet baking challenges. "If it has sugar, butter, eggs and flour...I'm your girl," she says.

The cookbook author has written two cookbooks for Renaissance Books, *Elegantly Easy Crème Brûlée* and *Elegantly Easy Liqueur Desserts*.

One dessert she hadn't tried, though, was a pianomo roll, a jelly-roll-style cake sold by a few local bakeries. The cake is remi-niscent of lady fingers and the filling is simple whipped butter. A dusting of sugar on the outside pretties it up.

As a test of her recipe-conjuring skills, Debbie came up with this formula, based on her tasting of the cake.

My daughter helped me bake one up and taste it side-by-side against a bakery cake. It was pretty darn close, and very simple to pull off.

Pianomo Roll

Makes 1 cake

5	egg yolks
1	teaspoon vanilla extract
¼	cup sugar
¾	cup cake flour, sifted twice

Meringue:

5	egg whites
¼	teaspoon cream of tartar
¼	teaspoon salt
¼	cup sugar

Filling:

¼	cup (½ stick) unsalted butter, slightly softened

Preheat oven to 375°F. Line a jelly-roll pan with waxed or parchment paper. In a large bowl, beat egg yolks, vanilla, and sugar until thick, about 5 minutes. Set aside.

To make Meringue: Using another bowl and clean beaters, beat egg whites, cream of tartar, and salt at high speed until soft peaks form. Gradually sprinkle in sugar until sugar dissolves and whites stand in stiff peaks.

Use a spatula to fold meringue into yolks, one-third at a time. Fold in flour, one-third at a time. Spread batter evenly in pan. Bake 10 to 12 minutes. Cake should be cooked in the center, but edges should not brown.

Sprinkle a clean dishcloth with sugar. Immediately invert hot cake onto dishcloth. Peel off parchment. Cool.

Meanwhile, whip butter at medium speed 5 minutes, until very fluffy. Spread evenly over cooled cake. Roll up cake jelly-roll fashion. When cake is sliced, the filling will show as a spiral through the cake.

June 2, 2004

It is difficult to imagine a child asking for a birthday prune cake, but that's probably just prejudice talking.

Prunes get a bad rap. It's that name: "Prune" just sounds like squishy, wrinkled, old-lady food. Or, worse, a stool-softener. Prune-makers have even come up with the new name of "dried plum" to get past all that.

This recipe turned up in response to a request from a reader whose mother always made her a prune cake for her birthday. She wanted to do the same for her kids. The recipe is from *Seasons of Baking 2*, a self-published cookbook from Henry Shun, a retired commercial baker.

Henry says the cake is reminiscent of those once served as wedding favors. If you can get past that fear of prunes, this is a moist and flavorful, not-too-sweet dessert. And if you can't get past it, Henry suggests trying the cake with other dried fruits, such as raisins, dates, figs or cranberries.

Prune Cake

Makes 1 cake

1 ½   cups plus 2 tablespoons cake flour
2   tablespoons bread flour (see note)
1   cup sugar
½   teaspoon salt
1   teaspoon baking soda
2   teaspoons baking powder
¾   cup vegetable oil
3   large or 4 medium eggs
1   teaspoon vanilla
2   teaspoons lemon juice
3   ounces chopped prunes (3/4 cup loosely packed)
½   cup plus 2 teaspoons milk
       Pinch cinnamon

Preheat oven to 365°F. Line bottom of an 8- or 9-inch-square cake pan with parchment paper. Do not grease.

Sift together flours, sugar, salt, baking soda, and baking powder.

Combine oil, eggs, vanilla, lemon juice, and prunes in a mixing bowl. Beat at low speed 3 minutes. Add dry ingredients and beat 4 minutes. Add milk and cinnamon, scrape sides of bowl and beat 1 more minute. Pour batter into pan. If desired, sprinkle a few more chopped prunes over top of cake.

Place pan on a cookie sheet (to keep bottom from darkening). Bake on center rack 30 to 35 minutes, or until cake is firm and leaves no indentation when touched. Cool, remove from pan, and wrap in plastic wrap. Let "age" 1 day for best flavor.

Note: All-purpose flour may be used in place of bread flour.

June 29, 2005

In places where it snows, a coconut cake is a warm-weather dessert, a reminder of the tropics, palm trees, and such.

Here in the land of eternal summer, we feel tropical all the time, so a coconut cake is less of a seasonal thing. Still, it does feel a lot more summery than, say, a pumpkin pie.

This version comes from Café Laufer in Kaimukī, courtesy of executive chef Cyrus Goo.

It's a light, layered chiffon with a coconut-custard filling and whipped-cream frosting. It's an advanced baking project, involving 21 (!) eggs—16 of which have to be separated—and custard-making. But it is well-worth the effort.

To save on labor (separating that many eggs can be a pain), buy pourable egg whites. In that case, make the custard with six whole eggs, rather than 16 yolks.

This recipe makes two 10-inch, triple-layer cakes. It is best to use springform pans, which have 3-inch-high sides.

As an alternative, you can use four 9-inch round cake pans, which will make two double-layer cakes. Or use two regular cake pans and use the leftover batter to make 24 cupcakes. Take them to work and be a hero. For best results, don't bake more than two cake pans or cupcake trays at a time.

Café Laufer Coconut Chiffon Cake

Makes 2 cakes

5	eggs
2	cups sugar
1	cup water
1	cup vegetable oil
3 ¾	cups cake flour, sifted
1	tablespoon baking powder
1	teaspoon salt
	Whipped cream, for frosting cake

Meringue:

16	egg whites
2	cups sugar

Custard:

4	cups milk, divided
2	cups sugar, divided
16	egg yolks (or 6 whole eggs)
½	cup cornstarch
1	cup whipped cream
3	cups grated coconut (fresh if possible)

To make Custard: Combine 3 cups milk with 1 cup sugar in a saucepan and bring to low boil over medium heat, stirring occasionally to prevent scorching.

Meanwhile, beat together egg yolks, cornstarch, and remaining milk and sugar. Add 1/4 cup of hot milk mixture to egg yolks and stir well. Slowly add all of egg mixture to hot milk; return to boil, stirring constantly. Cook, stirring, 2 minutes to remove starchy taste. Cool to room temperature, then refrigerate overnight.

Continued on next page

The next day, bake the cake: Whip together eggs and sugar just until incorporated. Combine water and oil; add to egg mixture. Stir to combine.

Combine cake flour, baking powder, and salt. Gradually add to egg mixture, stirring until well-combined.

Preheat oven to 350°F.

To make Meringue: Beat egg whites and sugar on high speed until medium peaks form (this will take at least 10 minutes). Pour into a large mixing bowl.

Fold batter into meringue. Pour into two ungreased 10-inch spring-form pans or four 9-inch round cake pans. Bake 30 minutes or until center springs back when touched.

Turn cake upside down onto a plate and cool on a rack. Release the springform catch and remove pan. If using regular cake pans, run a butter knife around the pans to loosen sides, then tap bottom of pans to release cakes.

Remove custard from refrigerator and add whipped cream, stirring to soften. Stir in half the coconut.

Cut each cake crosswise into thirds to make 3 layers per cake. Spread custard between layers. (If you used regular cake pans, no need to cut the cakes. Each one makes a layer, so you'll have 2 double-layer cakes.)

Frost cake with whipped cream and sprinkle with more coconut.

January 12, 2000

The Guava Chiffon Cake is a fusion dessert that's been around longer, probably, than the word "fusion" has been a trendy part of the culinary vocabulary.

A classic European cake fused with a tropical fruit, guava chiffon is an airy treat with a jelly-like filling that well represents local desserts.

The recipe was worked out via e-mail exchange with a reader who really, really wanted a guava chiffon to call her own. We both fussed around with the problem. What follows is a combination of her efforts and mine—the end result approximates a bakery guava chiffon.

This frosting is guava-flavored and pink, unlike the familiar white whipped-cream frosting. Add the topping and you have a triple dose of guava—well worth the work.

To simplify the process, this is designed as a single-layer cake that fits in a standard baking pan. If you want a more traditional look, cut the cake into layers and use a plain whipped-cream frosting. Use the topping in this recipe between the layers and perhaps as a drizzle on top.

DEAN SENSUI

Guava Chiffon Cake   Makes 1 cake

Batter:
2 ¾   cups cake flour
⅔   cup sugar
4   teaspoons baking powder
1   teaspoon salt
½   cup salad oil
½   cup water
¾   cup guava juice concentrate, thawed, undiluted
5   egg yolks, slightly beaten
2   teaspoons vanilla
2 to 3 drops red food coloring

Meringue:
7   egg whites
½   teaspoon cream of tartar
½   cup sugar

Guava Chiffon Frosting:
4   egg yolks
½   cup sugar
¾   cup guava juice concentrate, thawed, undiluted
1   cup whipping cream
¼   teaspoon vanilla

Guava Topping:
2   tablespoons cornstarch
½   cup water
       Pinch salt
1   12-ounce can guava juice
1   teaspoon lemon juice
1   slightly beaten egg yolk
1   tablespoon butter

Preheat oven to 325°F and lightly grease the bottom of an 11x 13-inch pan.

To make Batter: Sift together cake flour, sugar, baking powder, and salt.

Make a well in the center; add oil, water, guava juice, egg yolks, and vanilla. Beat with a spoon until mixture is smooth. Add food coloring. Set aside.

To make Meringue: Beat egg whites with cream of tartar until soft peaks form. Gradually beat in 1/2 cup sugar until stiff.

Gently fold batter into meringue until barely mixed. Pour into pan. Bake 35 to 40 minutes, until a pick inserted in the center comes out clean. Remove from oven and invert on a rack to cool completely.

To make Guava Chiffon Frosting: Beat egg yolks and sugar until lemon-colored; add guava juice, place in saucepan, and cook over low to medium heat until thick, about 8 minutes. Remove from heat and chill.

Whip cream and vanilla, then fold into guava mixture.

To make Guava Topping: Mix cornstarch with water in a saucepan. Stir to dissolve lumps. Add salt, guava, and lemon juices, and egg yolk. Cook over low heat until thick, stirring constantly. Remove from heat and add butter. Cool slightly.

To assemble cake: Remove carefully from pan. Frost sides of cake with guava frosting. Cover top with guava topping (it's easier to spread if still warm).

Note: To turn this into a layer cake, cut the 9 x 13-inch cake in half. Chill the cake, then spread the bottom layer with the guava topping. Chill it again to firm everything up before adding the top layer. Cover with whipped cream, then spread or drizzle more topping on top. If you wish to use the guava frosting from this recipe instead of whipped cream, double the recipe.

August 30, 2000

Back in the days before Hawai'i Regional Cuisine, there were three Hawaiian flavors: pineapple, coconut, and macadamia nut. That's it. Pau.

"Hawaiian" dishes from fifteen or more years ago tended to dance around those tastes. That's not necessarily bad. Some of these classics are firmly seated in the nostalgia part of our taste buds.

For example, the *Hawai'i Five-O* Torte, named for the TV show. It was printed in the *Star-Bulletin* many years ago.

The original torte called for pecans in the crust, but I'd use mac nuts, because what the heck, we're in a Hawaiiana mode. Also, do not be alarmed at the 500°F baking temperature for the final step of browning the meringue. You turn off the oven before putting in the torte and nothing burns. The original recipe called for leaving it in the oven for a nonspecific "several hours"; I found that 30 minutes yields good results.

Hawai'i Five-O Torte

Makes 1 torte

Crust:
1   cup flour
½   cup butter
⅓   cup chopped pecans or macadamia nuts
⅓   cup flaked coconut

Filling:
1   can (1-pound, 4-ounces) unsweetened crushed pineapple
1   envelope unflavored gelatin
1   2.9-ounce package lemon pudding and pie filling mix
¼   cup water
½   cup sugar
3   egg yolks
1   cup sour cream

Meringue:

3   egg whites

¼   teaspoon cream of tartar

1 ¼ cups sifted powdered sugar

Preheat oven to 350°F.

To make Crust: Cut flour into butter, then add nuts and coconut; blend to crumb consistency. Press into an 8-inch square pan and bake for 20 minutes. Remove pan and cool.

To make Filling: Drain juice from pineapple and set fruit aside. Add water to juice to make 2 cups. Soften gelatin in 1/4 cup water.

Combine lemon pie filling, water, sugar, and egg yolks in a medium saucepan. Mix until smooth. Add pineapple juice mixture and combine well. Bring to a boil over medium heat, stirring constantly. Cook 2 minutes, until smooth and thick, stirring constantly. Remove from heat; stir in softened gelatin. Fold in drained pineapple. Cool 10 minutes.

Preheat oven to 500°F.

Remove filling from refrigerator; fold in sour cream and turn into cooled crust.

To make Meringue: Beat egg whites with cream of tartar. Gradually beat in powdered sugar until very stiff.

Cover torte with meringue. Place in oven and turn heat off. Leave in oven for about 30 minutes, or until meringue is nicely browned. Remove torte and sift powdered sugar over the top. Chill well, until filling is set.

November 8, 2000

The usual coconut pie is a creamy thing, which makes this Coconut Macaroon Pie something unique for the dessert table.

The reader who asked for the recipe remembered the pie as it was served at the Honolulu Community College bakeshop a couple decades ago. Finding it took some asking around, as the HCC bakeshop closed several years ago. But one of the chef-instructors, Isaac Tamada, turned up on Lāna'i, at the Manele Bay and Lodge at Koele.

Isaac taught at HCC for twelve years, and saved one copy of the recipe book prepared for HCC students.

The original dessert probably dates to the 1960s, Isaac said, but was still going strong when he got to the school in the 1980s. "It's very simple and yet nice eating."

The pie uses macaroon coconut, which is NOT the same as shredded baker's coconut that you'll find at the grocery store. Macaroon coconut is dried and comes in tiny flakes. If you can't find it at your market, try a health-food store.

Coconut Macaroon Pie

Makes 1 pie

1	cup sugar
2	tablespoons plus 1/2 teaspoon cornstarch
2	cups water
⅛	teaspoon almond extract
2	cups macaroon coconut
1	teaspoon butter
1	Prepared double crust for an 8-inch pie

Preheat oven to 350°F.

Combine sugar and cornstarch. Add water and almond extract. Cook over medium heat until mixture comes to a boil. Remove from heat and stir in coconut. Cool to room temperature.

Pour filling into pie crust and dab butter around filling. Cover with top crust and seal. Make slits in the top crust or a single hole in the center to vent steam. Bake 40 minutes, or until crust is golden or filling can be seen bubbling through the center hole.

August 13, 2003

Toffee is a hard candy made with butter and sugar, often paired with chocolate and nuts for a winning combination of softness, richness, and crunch (think of a Health candy bar).

A Chocolate Coffee-Toffee Pie replicates the flavor, if not the texture, through a creamy filling of butter, sugar, and melted chocolate, with coffee stirred in for good measure.

One warning: This crust can be very difficult to dig out of the pie pan, so grease very well. You could also simplify matters by substituting a standard graham cracker crust.

Or, dispense with a crust altogether—the filling is so good it could be served alone as a mousse. But note that the filling contains two raw eggs. To limit the risk of salmonella, the pie should be kept well-chilled. Use care if serving the dish to anyone at particular risk (very young children, the elderly, or those with compromised immune systems).

Chocolate Coffee-Toffee Pie

Makes 1 pie

Crust:

1	cup flour
½	cup (1 stick) butter, softened
¼	cup light brown sugar, lightly packed
1	ounce (1 square) unsweetened chocolate, grated
1	teaspoon vanilla extract
2	tablespoons water
¾	cup finely chopped walnuts or pecans

Filling:

½	cup (1 stick) butter, softened
¾	cup sugar
2	teaspoons powdered instant coffee
1	ounce (1 square) unsweetened chocolate, melted
2	eggs

Preheat oven to 375°F. Grease a 9-inch pie pan very well.

To make Crust: Combine flour, butter, brown sugar, and chocolate using a pastry cutter or by hand. Add vanilla, water, and nuts. Use hands to mix dough until it holds together in a ball. Add a few drops more water if necessary. Press dough into pie pan by hand. Prick all over with a fork. Bake 15 minutes. Cool.

To make Filling: Beat butter on high speed until fluffy. Gradually beat in sugar. Beat in instant coffee and melted chocolate. Add 1 egg; beat on high speed 5 minutes. Add second egg and beat 5 more minutes. Spread filling in cooled pie shell. Cover and refrigerate several hours, until firm. Top with whipped cream.

September 16, 1998

The bread pudding at Agnes' Portuguese Bake Shop in Kailua is a rich blend of sweetbread, apples, raisins, and spices. Chief baker Non DeMello says the key is not so much the recipe as the execution—mixing well without overmixing, for example.

For that reason, he's free with the recipe.

Agnes, by the way, was Agnes Wright, who, with her husband Tommy, was the original owner of the bakery. Non and his partner bought the bakery from the Wrights' son-in-law eleven years ago.

Non says a fat analysis of his bread pudding would be "scary." He offers ways to trim the fat: Try using egg whites only, fat-free evaporated milk, coconut flavoring instead of shredded coconut, and eliminate the butter.

But Non warns that it won't taste the same. His bread pudding is simply not for the calorie-squeamish. It's like buying a Jaguar, he says: "If you have to ask the price, you can't afford it." And if you have to ask for the fat content of his bread pudding, you can't afford the calories.

DENNIS ODA

Agnes' Portuguese Bake Shop Bread Pudding   Serves 12

1	1-pound Portuguese sweetbread loaf, in ½-inch cubes
1 ½	cups raisins
⅓	cup flaked coconut, preferably unsweetened
¾	cup peeled, cored, and chopped apple
¼	cup butter or margarine, melted
2	cups evaporated milk
2	cups water
2	cups sugar
4	eggs
2	tablespoons cinnamon
2	teaspoons ground ginger
1	teaspoon nutmeg
½	teaspoon salt
1	cup brown sugar, lightly packed

DENNIS ODA

Preheat oven to 350°F to 375°F.

Combine bread, raisins, coconut, and apple. Drizzle butter over mixture and lightly toss.

In a separate bowl, whisk together the evaporated milk, water, sugar, eggs, cinnamon, ginger, nutmeg, and salt, making sure the sugar is completely dissolved.

Pour liquid mixture into the bread mixture. Stir to combine, but do not overmix (don't let bread cubes get too soggy).

Allow mix to sit about 15 minutes. Pour into a greased 9 x 13-inch pan. Spread brown sugar evenly over the top.

Place pan into a larger pan filled with water. Bake 50 minutes to 1 hour, until the pudding has "puffed" a little and springs back to the touch. Cool before cutting. Refrigerate leftovers.

June 6, 2001

The holy grail for many local bakers is a chantilly frosting like the sweet, buttery concoction made by Liliha Bakery. It tops chocolate cakes and Liliha's famous Coco Puffs.

Chantilly frosting of this style is a very local creation. Classic French chantilly is made of sweetened whipping cream, sometimes flavored with nuts, toasted coconut, fruit, mint, or maple sugar.

What we know as chantilly, however, is a butter cream frosting, maple colored and very smooth.

Liliha Bakery's Chantilly Cake—chocolate, with the signature frosting (but no nuts) is the second most popular item, after the Coco Puff. President William Takakuwa closely guards recipes, but he does allow that it is basically a German chocolate cake frosting, without the nuts and coconut, and with a whole lot of butter added.

Getting it exactly the same would take hours of experimentation, but here is an approximation. It's not the Liliha formula, but it is tasty. The key is to cook the frosting in a double boiler—not direct heat—for smoothness. Also, use real butter, not margarine, and fully fatted evaporated milk, not skim.

Chantilly Cake Frosting

Makes enough to
frost a 9 x 13-inch cake
or two 8-inch layers

1   cup evaporated milk
1   cup white sugar
3   egg yolks, beaten
½   cup butter
1   teaspoon vanilla extract

Optional:

1 ⅓   cups flaked coconut and/or 1 cup chopped macadamia nuts

Combine milk, sugar, egg yolks, butter, and vanilla in the top portion of a double boiler, or in a bowl placed over a saucepan of boiling water.

Cook over medium heat until thick, about 12 minutes, stirring constantly to keep the eggs from scrambling and the frosting from clumping.

Remove from heat. Add coconut and/or nuts if desired. Cool, stirring occasionally, until thick enough to spread.

April 13, 2005

B rian Jahnke, manager of the Wai'oli Tea Room, has a memory that goes way, way back—and a recipe collection to match.

This proved to be good news for a reader who had been nursing a craving for the date bars that she enjoyed at the tea room—she guesses thirty years ago. "I've been haunted by this recipe for years," she wrote.

It's easy to see why, once you've baked up a batch. These bars are soft, chewy, and just sweet enough.

If you've been to the Wai'oli Tea Room lately, note that these are not the bars currently on the menu; they come from a generation ago.

It's a simple recipe. My only caution is to resist the urge to cut into them too soon. They are very soft right out of the oven and need time to set up.

Wai'oli Tea Room Date Bars

Makes 12 bars

Filling:

2	cups chopped dates
½	cup brown sugar
1	cup water
1	tablespoon flour
4	teaspoons vanilla

Crust:

1 ¼	cups flour, sifted
1	teaspoon baking soda
3	cups old-fashioned rolled oats
1	cup brown sugar
1	cup butter, melted

To make Filling: Combine all ingredients except vanilla in a saucepan and simmer over medium-low heat until dates are soft and mixture thickens, 3 to 4 minutes. Cool. Stir in vanilla.

Preheat oven to 350°F. Lightly grease an 8- or 9-inch baking pan.

Combine flour, baking soda, oats, and sugar. Mix well.

Add butter and stir to combine. Press half the crust mixture into the bottom of pan. Spread date filling evenly over bottom crust. Top with remaining crust and press gently into an even layer. Bake 35 to 40 minutes, until top is lightly toasted.

Cool completely before cutting.

May 29, 2002

I spent Memorial Day playing with chocolate. There are worse ways to spend a holiday.

I was looking for a chocolate sauce that hardens when poured on ice cream, and the only way to guarantee results was to try out a few recipes and taste. Repeatedly.

We now have a half-dozen chocolate-covered strawberries in the refrigerator, quite a bit of French vanilla ice cream in the freezer (standing by for further testing, of course) and three types of leftover chocolate sauce.

The solution turned out to be quite simple. It came from Mark Okumura, pastry chef for Alan Wong's restaurants.

It has just two ingredients: bittersweet chocolate, which is easy to find in supermarkets, and cocoa butter, which is not. Pure cocoa butter is sold at Hans Weiler in Kalihi (847-2210), in a 4-ounce jar marked "natural moisturizer," but do not be alarmed. It is 100 percent edible, with the added benefit of moisturizing skin, which gives you something to do with the leftovers. A jar costs $5.90 and is enough to make 2 pounds of chocolate sauce.

Mark's recipe also can be used to dip ice cream bars or frozen bananas. And it makes beautiful chocolate-dipped strawberries.

Hard Chocolate Sauce

Makes about 3/4 cup

4   ounces bittersweet chocolate, broken in pieces
1   ounce cocoa butter

Melt chocolate and cocoa butter together over a double boiler, stirring until smooth. Sauce may be used immediately or after cooling slightly.

Pour over ice cream to create a hard chocolate shell. Dip ice cream bars or frozen bananas in sauce. Dip strawberries or other fruit (oranges are especially good) in sauce and place on a plate lined with waxed paper. Refrigerate until chocolate hardens.

August 10, 2005

Took the kids to the Hawai'i State Farm Fair last weekend and came across something I had thought to be urban legend—the Fried Twinkie®.

I'd read about these, but never actually confronted one. The idea always seemed way too audacious and, well, greasy.

But, in this job, I've learned you must give all edible creations at least one try. This has led to many adventures: Veal cheeks (yum), natto (yuck), sea urchin (depends on the circumstances).

Fried Twinkies® turned out to be a revelation. Crunchy on the outside, soft and creamy on the inside—and they don't even taste like Twinkies®. Lots of recipes can be found for this treat; this one is based on my home-testing. One tip: To decrease the grease, remove Twinkies® from the hot pot with tongs and tap the tongs sharply on the side of the pot to shake off excess oil.

Fried Twinkie®

Makes 6

6   Twinkies®, frozen
     Vegetable oil for deep-frying
     Powdered sugar

Batter:
1   cup flour
1   tablespoon malt vinegar
1   teaspoon baking powder
1   teaspoon salt
1 ½ cups water

Heat oil to 375°F.

Combine batter ingredients and mix until smooth. Dip Twinkies® in batter and fry until golden brown, about 90 seconds. Sprinkle with powdered sugar.

February 23, 2005

The Rice Krispie® Treat has a counterpart in the Japanese repertoire, a snack that's just as crunchy, but not as sweet.

It's called okoshi, and it's made with puffed wheat or rice cereal. Not Rice Krispies®, but another dry cereal—the common brand is Quaker Oats®. The cereal is a little like puffed rice on steroids—bigger and fatter.

When first printed, this recipe posed some problems for readers, who complained that something had to be wrong with it. I've concluded that the problem is bulk. Common okoshi recipes call for 10 cups of cereal, which conveniently uses up a whole box. But that quantity is difficult to work with.

At this size, it's still a bit tricky, but much more manageable, and it does make a good, light okoshi.

Once you get the hang of it, you can use the rest of the box of cereal, perhaps adding more peanuts or more sauce, to taste.

Perfectly shaped bars will come only with practice. For now, settle for a random, homemade look.

Okoshi

5	cups puffed wheat or rice cereal (see note)
¼	cup roasted peanuts
¾	block butter
¾	cup sugar

Preheat oven to 200°F. Set out a large bowl, large cookie sheet, and a spatula. Coat all 3 with cooking oil spray. Set out a small bowl of ice water.

Spread cereal and peanuts in a pan and place in oven.

Melt butter over medium heat, then add sugar. Stir continuously. The butter will brown slightly and the sugar will melt into a clear liquid. As you stir, the substances will combine to form a smooth caramel-like sauce. This will take about 5 minutes. Remove from heat.

Quickly remove cereal and peanuts from oven and pour into greased bowl. Stir sauce again, then drizzle quickly over cereal mix. Stir with greased spatula to coat cereal. Speed is of the essence here; the sauce hardens quickly and will become difficult to handle. If possible, have someone stir while you pour and scrape the pot of all the sauce.

Turn cereal onto greased cookie sheet and use hands to press mixture flat and push in sides to form a firm block, about 1 inch thick. If mixture is hot to touch, dip fingers in ice water so you can keep working. Some cereal will escape (and probably fall on the floor); can't help that.

Cut or break into pieces while still warm.

Note: The common brand of puffed cereal is Quaker Oats®. It is not found in all supermarkets, but I did find it at Daiei.

November 18, 1998

Twenty-five years ago, the ladies of the Hongwanji struck gold. A dozen of them hit on the idea of publishing a cookbook, featuring the tried-and-true recipes of members of their temple, the Honpa Hongwanji Hawai'i Betsuin.

They collected more than 200 recipes, typed them up, printed them on the office "printing machine" (not as good as a photocopier, not as bad as a ditto machine) and punched holes in the pages.

Every Sunday, before and after services, men, women, and children collated the pages and bound the books—2,500 to 3,000 copies—the collective memory is a bit hazy on the exact number.

The price was $3.50 and they were afraid the books wouldn't sell. But *Favorite Island Cookery,* now known as *Cookbook I*, was a sell out. In fact, some people got upset when the stock ran out. They had to turn to a commercial printer to keep up with demand.

At the time—1973—local cookbooks were rare and *Island Cookery*, with its recipes taken straight from island homes, struck a chord.

Five more editions followed over the years as the cookbooks became a major income source for the Betsuin—$72,000 raised since 1991 (records are vague before then).

Other churches, schools, and community organizations took up the idea, to the point where today, these kinds of cookbooks are everywhere.

If there were a game called Stump the Cook, local-style, the reference book to decide all challenges would be *Island Cookery.*

A request for Chinese-style peanut candy, that chewy, peanut-sesame candy bar, was surely an attempt to stump the cook, but the recipe is right there on page 194 of *Book VI*, latest in the series, circa 1995.

It looks simple, but getting just the right chewy texture is tricky. Exact cooking time is the key and you may have to try a few times to get it right. If you don't cook the syrup long enough, your candy will be too soft; cook too long and you have peanut brittle. Believe me, I did it both ways.

Sesame Peanut Candy

2	cups sugar
⅙	cup vinegar
⅙	cup water
½	cup toasted sesame seeds
1 ½	cups roasted, unsalted peanuts

Heat sugar, vinegar, and water in a saucepan over low heat, stirring until sugar dissolves. Cook without stirring until mixture boils, then boil until syrup reaches a soft golden brown, 10 to 15 minutes.

Meanwhile, grease an 11 x 7-inch pan or line it with cookie parchment. Sprinkle half the sesame seeds and all of the peanuts over the bottom of the pan. Pour syrup over nuts; smooth surface with a greased wooden spoon. Sprinkle with remaining sesame seeds. Cool, cutting into pieces when still slightly warm.

May 5, 1999

This recipe is designed to make your mouth water, literally. It comes from my mother, Betty Zane Shimabukuro, a retired home economist. (She once told me that I was named for her and she was named for Betty Boop. It's a dubious distinction).

She has a voluminous collection of recipes—many of them (like this Prune Mui recipe) preserved on handwritten index cards.

If you try it, be prepared to pucker up.

DENNIS ODA

Prune Mui

1	pound light brown sugar
2	tablespoons Hawaiian salt
3	tablespoons whiskey
1	teaspoon Chinese 5-spice
10	whole cloves
1 ½	cups lemon juice
6	ounces preserved lemons
4	ounces seedless li hing mui
6	pounds prunes

Mix ingredients and place in a large glass jar. Soak at least 4 days, turning the jar over twice a day.

July 28, 1999

Three babies and a cookbook. When Teresa De-Virgilio-Lam gave birth 2-1/2 years ago, that's what she got. The babies—triplets, three little girls—are Gabrielle, Ashlyn, and Alexis. The cookbook—born during three months of bed rest at the end of the pregnancy—is *Unbearably Good! Mochi Lovers' Cookbook*, Morris Press, 1999, $7.95.

DeVirgilio-Lam has been collecting mochi recipes since childhood. These come from friends and family.

Cocoa Mochi

2	cups mochiko
1 ¾	cups sugar
3	tablespoons cocoa powder
1	tablespoon baking soda
2	eggs, beaten
1	12-ounce can evaporated milk
1	can coconut milk
¼	cup melted butter
1	teaspoon vanilla

Preheat oven to 350°F.

Sift together mochiko, sugar, cocoa, and baking soda. Add eggs, milk, coconut milk, butter, and vanilla. Mix until smooth. Pour into a greased and floured 9 x 13-inch pan. Bake 1 hour and 10 minutes. Cool before slicing.

Butter Mochi

1	pound mochiko
2 ½	cups sugar
1	teaspoon baking powder
3	cups milk
5	eggs, beaten
1	teaspoon vanilla
½	cup butter, melted and cooled
1	cup shredded coconut

Preheat oven to 350°F.

Combine mochiko, sugar, and baking powder. Add milk, eggs, vanilla, butter, and coconut to dry ingredients and mix well. Pour into a greased 9 x 13-inch pan. Bake 1 hour. Cool before slicing.

April 21, 2004

Arare has always come into my house ready-made. Just like, say, shoes. I understand it is theoretically possible to make your own shoes, but how? And why?

Same for arare—also known as mochi crunch or kaki mochi—that slightly salty, ever crunchy Japanese rice cracker. This snack food is certainly cheap enough to buy in large quantity, and its quality, mass-production aside, rarely seems an issue.

But I have found that for every edible substance there is a person who wants to make it from scratch. And somewhere, there is a recipe.

The arare process turns out to be pretty simple, although tedious. The ingredients are cheap—mochiko, sugar, sesame seeds, soy sauce, corn syrup—so if you have the time, it's a worthy adventure.

Why? Well, because you can.

Besides, it's kind of magical, making arare. Examine a handful—the specific culinary process is not clear. Unlike a cookie, which is obviously baked, or a potato chip, which is obviously fried, arare seems the product of some other process.

Turns out it is both fried and baked, first to get it light and puffy, second to bake on a sweet-salty glaze.

First, though, you have to form the pieces, by rolling out a simple dough and cutting it. This is a critical step in the recipe: Roll the dough out paper thin and cut into half-inch pieces. My first batch was too thick. The dog enjoyed it, though.

This recipe calls for cutting out simple squares using a knife, which maximizes the dough. You could make fancier shapes such as flowers using canapé cutters, but it's probably best in the beginning if you don't get too cocky.

I thought the real tricky part was going to be frying, but as long as you get the oil to the right temperature (375°F), the dough does just what it's supposed to—rises to the surface, puffs up and turns golden. It won't be crisp yet, so don't think that anything's wrong.

The part where judgment and technique come in is in the glazing. You need to cook a mixture of soy sauce, corn syrup, and sugar on the stovetop just enough to thicken slightly. Cook too long and it'll be too thick to coat evenly.

The coated arare goes in the oven, and again, only experience will get you to the point where you can declare success. If you rush, your arare will be sticky and not quite crunchy. Bake too long and it'll taste burnt. It's hard to eyeball the process because the glaze makes it very dark from the start. You need to check an individual piece for that elu-sive state of "almost done." The glaze will be set, but the arare won't be quite crunchy—that comes when it completely cools.

Best solution: Glaze and bake in small batches until you have the baking time right for your oven. The good news is, even when burnt this arare tastes pretty good. Did I mention I made several batches?

Ready? Good luck.

Japanese Rice Crackers

Makes about 100 rice crackers

¾   cup flour
¾   cup mochiko
1 ½ tablespoons sugar
1   tablespoon black sesame seeds
1   teaspoon baking powder
½   cup water
      Vegetable oil for frying

Glaze:
¼   cup corn syrup
¼   cup sugar
¼   cup soy sauce

Combine flour, mochiko, sugar, sesame seeds, baking powder, and water to make a smooth dough. Add a little more water if dough is too dry.

Flour work surface lightly with mochiko. Roll out dough in small batches. Dough must be very thin, almost paper-thin. Use a knife to cut into 1/2-inch squares.

Heat oil to 375°F.

Fry crackers in batches until golden brown on both sides. This will take just a few seconds. Remove with a slotted spoon or strainer, tapping the sides of the fryer to remove excess oil. Drain on paper towels.

Preheat oven to 300°F. Place cooled rice crackers on a cookie sheet.

To make Glaze: Combine corn syrup, sugar, and soy sauce in a pan and bring to a boil over medium heat. Cook until sugar dissolves and mixture begins to thicken, about a minute. Do not overcook or the glaze will be difficult to spread.

Pour glaze over rice crackers and mix to coat evenly. Work quickly, as glaze will harden as it cools. Spread crackers into a single layer and separate pieces. Bake 15 to 20 minutes, until glaze is set and crackers are dry but not quite crisp. They will harden and get crispy as they cool. Do not over bake or glaze will burn.

Five Special Stories

Much of newspaper reporting is a matter of figuring out what you need to know, finding someone who knows it, getting them to tell you what they know, and writing it down.

People can help you or not. In my case, they can cough up their recipes or not.

I would like to close this collection with a bit of self-indulgence. A thank you to a few chefs who've been especially generous in sharing their skills. I consider them all to be great at what they do—and after all the times I've bothered them, I consider them rare friends as well.

Hiroshi Fukui, Hiroshi Eurasian Tapas

When I take people to eat at Hiroshi's for the first time, there's always a moment when they'll take a bite and freeze. It's gotten so I'll watch for it to happen.

Hiroshi's food will do this to you. He's got some magical, masterful way of balancing clean, striking flavors so a sauce brightens and completes a dish without overpowering it.

When readers write in to ask for his recipes, they'll mention these almost spiritual encounters with his food. One woman said she took one taste of his ponzu butter sauce and "my eyes rolled back in my head."

Hiroshi was one of the first friends I made when I started writing about food—lucky for me. His advice has saved me all kinds of time researching Japanese cooking. (Once he even called another restaurant for me and got a recipe out of a cook who didn't speak English.)

Hiroshi was born in Yokohama, Japan. His mother was Japanese; his father, a shipboard cook from Maui. At age 12, in

KATHRYN BENDER

1977, he moved to Hawaiʻi with his father, after losing his mother to stomach cancer.

He remains fluent in Japanese; English was learned in an American school in Japan. He says when he entered Kaimukī Intermediate School, the kids made fun of his schoolboy English, so as a matter of self-defense he became fluent in pidgin. Talk to him now and you'd think he was born here.

He started in restaurants as a dishwasher at Furusato Japanese Restaurant, so far down the pecking order that he rarely got to sample the dishes. "What you do is stand by the dishwasher and just when they're about to throw out the food, that's when you get your taste."

Still, he picked up an interest in cooking and eventually worked his way through the intensely structured Japanese model: two to three years at various stations—pantry, tempura, grill, up to the ultimate position of handling sashimi.

Hiroshi's food is not traditionally Japanese, though. It is a merger of Japanese and European techniques—in foodie circles it's called Eurasian—but he does it in a way that's never fussy or silly.

Whatever name eventually falls to this cuisine—new wave, neo-Japanese, Japanese-with-a-twist—it is a limitless source of challenge and opportunity.

"If you think about it, the variations of Japanese and European flavors, there's no end to it," Hiroshi says. "You can keep creating."

Dashi
Makes 6 cups

6   cups cold water
1   (6-inch) piece dashi konbu (dried kelp), rinsed quickly in cold water
1   cup katsuobushi (dried bonito flakes)

Place water and konbu in a pot over high heat. Remove konbu just before water comes to a boil. Stir in katsuobushi and turn off heat. Let sit 2 minutes, until katsuobushi settles in bottom of pan.

Skim and strain stock.

Kīlauea Tofu

Serves 4

1	block tofu
1	cup katakuriko (potato starch)
	Vegetable oil for frying

Sauce:

18	ounces (2-¼ cups) dashi (recipe opposite)
3	ounces (6 tablespoons) mirin
3	ounces (6 tablespoons) light soy sauce
1	teaspoon sugar
1	teaspoon Thai chili sauce
3	teaspoons katakuriko (potato starch), dissolved in 2 teaspoons water
½	cup sliced mushrooms, mix of oyster and shiitake
¼	cup sliced bell peppers, mix of green, red, yellow

Garnish:

Katsuobushi (bonito flakes)
Diced chives
Grated ginger

Cut tofu into 8 blocks. Drain well on paper towels.

Dredge tofu pieces lightly in potato starch. Heat oil to 350°F and fry tofu until light brown and crispy.

To make Sauce: Combine dashi, mirin, soy sauce, sugar and chile sauce in a saucepan and bring to a boil. Stir in katakuriko slurry, adding it a little at a time and stirring as sauce thickens. Once sauce is thick enough to coat a spoon, add mushrooms and bell peppers.

Serve tofu with sauce, topped with garnishes.

Note: If making the sauce ahead, leave out vegetables. Sauce may be kept, refrigerated, up to 2 days. Bring to a boil and add vegetables.

Thomas Ky, Assaggio

My favorite restaurant story in all of Hawai'i is the story of Thomas Ky and the Assaggio chain.

Thomas is the kind of guy who makes you feel as though you've been standing still your entire life. His time in this country has been a treadmill of hard work and hard-won achievement, beginning the day his parents put him on a tiny boat and sent him away from Vietnam, carrying the family's future. He was 14.

Many immigrant stories begin this way—in youth, in poverty, in loneliness in a strange land. Thomas Ky's story is extraordinary for how totally he has overcome all that, to become a player in perhaps Hawai'i's toughest business.

Barely twenty years since stepping onto that boat, speaking no English, carrying no cash, Thomas owns four thriving Italian restaurants.

He worked in restaurants while in high school, then afterward worked two or three jobs to build up his savings. Every month he'd put $1,000 in the bank and sent a few hundred more home to Vietnam. When he had $16,000 he opened his first restaurant, Salerno in McCully Shopping Center. He sold his interest in Salerno in 1991, and that became the seed money for the first Assagio, in Kailua.

In 1995, Thomas was able to bring his parents and four brothers and sisters out of Vietnam—and to his new home in Wai'alae Iki.

Tell him his story is remarkable, though, and Thomas insists he could see no other way. "Sometimes there is no choice. Either you die or you go and live...Sometimes it's not too fair. But life is not fair."

Priorities are different when your goal for so many years has been to get your family away from the Communists.

Thomas has always been very generous with recipes, even for Assaggio's most popular signature dishes. He once told me it was silly for restaurants to guard their recipes so closely that they won't share.

Chicken Assaggio

Serves 2

6	ounces fresh island chicken, boned, in strips 1/4-inch wide
1	tablespoon extra virgin olive oil
⅛	teaspoon dry basil
	Salt and pepper to taste
2	cloves garlic, chopped
¾	cup pepperoncini, diced
1	cup roasted bell peppers
1	tablespoon capers
¾	cup button mushrooms
18	medium black olives
½	cup dry white wine
2	tablespoons butter
5	ounces fresh linguine, cooked

GEORGE F. LEE

Preheat oven to 350°F.

Sear chicken in olive oil in an oven-proof skillet; add salt, pepper, and basil. Bake 5 minutes, or until chicken is cooked through.

Return pan to stove top and add garlic, pepperoncini, bell pepper, capers, mushrooms, olives, and wine. Sauté 1 minute, then add butter. Stir until sauce thickens, then serve on a bed of linguine.

Chef Chai Chaowasaree, Chai's Island Bistro

Hands down the most interesting thing I've ever written about came as the result of a conversation with Chai. He was all excited, telling me how he'd been looking for years for a black chicken—and had finally found a steady supply.

The silkie chicken—that's its official name—has been around for generations, renowned for healing properties throughout Asia. Chai remembers his father and grandfather preparing soup with black chickens in his native Thailand.

It is a very distinctive bird. Thanks to a recessive gene, the silkie has an extra toe—five instead of the usual four—and it has fluffy "barbless" feathers. The feathers may be black or white; the earlobes, interestingly enough, are turquoise.

Plucked of its feathers, though, the silkie goes from extremely cute to extremely bizarre. It is a deep charcoal color from top to bottom, beak to toenails—and inside-out, from skin to bones. The cooked meat is gray with black streaks. Sliced, it resembles oysters, or large mushrooms.

The meat is very lean, not at all gamy, and is normally served in soups or stews. In Asia it is believed to have medicinal qualities.

Perhaps black chicken soup is the secret to Chai's seemingly endless stores of energy. The guy is doing everything, all the time—television show, charity events, restaurant management. Still, he has

always had the time to answer my ignorant questions about Thai cooking—always accessible and quick to share. Once he walked me through the whole process of extracting tamarind juice over the phone.

Anyway, for these black chickens: In Hawai'i they seem to be a delicacy of past generations, but they are available in some Chinatown stores and at 99 Ranch Market.

Chai says extracting the full benefit requires long, slow cooking. His method is similar to poaching, letting the chicken sit immersed in liquid over very low heat.

"You don't want to rush the heat; you want all the nutrition to come out slowly, slowly, slowly."

His soup uses ginseng, ginger, and garlic, also believed to have healing qualities and which lend the broth a peppery flavor. Don't bother peeling the ginseng or ginger, he says, and use whole heads of garlic, leaving the paper skins in place.

KEN IGE

Black Chicken Soup

1   silkie chicken (about 2 pounds), whole or halved
3   thumb-sized pieces ginseng root
6 ¼   cups water
1   thumb-sized piece ginger, smashed
2   large heads garlic, halved
½   teaspoon whole peppercorns
     Salt or soy sauce to taste
5   dried figs
     Sliced green onion for garnish

Cut chicken in half if necessary to fit pot; otherwise leave whole. Soak ginseng in water 1 hour.

Place ginseng and its soaking water in pot; add chicken, ginger, garlic, pepper, and salt. Bring to a boil and skim impurities. Reduce heat to a very low simmer (no bubbling at all) and cook until chicken is fall-off-the-bone tender, 2 to 4 hours. Or cook in a crock pot on low heat, about 6 hours. In last hour of cooking, add figs.

Strain soup and debone chicken if desired, or serve with root pieces. Garnish with green onion.

Colin Nishida, Side Street Inn

DENNIS ODA

The godfather of Side Street Inn is Colin Nishida, who has managed to create a somewhat surreal space where the food has grown legendary and where sports fans, off-duty professionals, and stressed-out restaurant magnates alike can eat, drink, and sing karaoke in total relaxation.

That was his goal coming in: "Build a local bar with good food, good service. A safe bar where women and men could come in. Not a hostess bar, not really a men's bar, not really a women's bar."

Not exactly a definitive mission statement, but, by any measure, Colin has succeeded.

Colin and I were once paired up in a cooking contest. We made a roast duck and foie gras dish—actually, Colin made it. My whole contribution was to tie up little bundles of herbs for decoration. We won, though, and I got to bask in the glory.

Side Street—and Colin's second restaurant, Fort Street Grill, are all about basic bar-and-grill food, done extremely well. That he can also pull off roast duck and foie gras proves he really knows what he's doing.

This despite no formal cooking training, other than that provided by his mother—"Gotta learn to cook rice. Come home from school, cook rice."

In the beginning, his menu had five items—teri chicken, fried rice, yaki soba, New York steak, and a fifth item Colin can't remember.

Side Street has grown from hideaway bar to honest-to-God restaurant. Colin now sells 300 to 400 pounds of pork chops a week (the recipe for that dish is among my Top Five Requests and is included in Chapter 1 of this book).

On the personal side: Colin's family is "six dogs and a girlfriend. She's very patient." And his mother, who still makes all Side Street's wonton.

Side Street Fried Rice

Serves 4

4	cups cooked rice
½	cup Portuguese sausage, diced
2	slices bacon, diced
½	cup green onions, chopped
½	cup frozen peas and carrots, thawed
½	cup char siu, chopped
¼	cup oyster sauce
1	teaspoon salt
2	tablespoons hon dashi (see note)

Dry rice in the refrigerator or freezer 1 day.

Brown sausage and bacon in a large skillet. Add rice and mix well. Add onions, peas, carrots, and char siu; mix. Add oyster sauce, salt, and hon dashi.

Note: For those sensitive to msg, use a saimin or shrimp dashi that has no msg. Leave out salt.

Jackie Lau, corporate chef, Roy's Restaurants in Hawai'i

You have to dig to find Jackie Lau's Mexican roots—past her Chinese married name (Lau), past her German maiden name (Groth) to her mother's family name (Flores).

Lau was schooled in Mexican cooking by three generations of Flores women—her mother, grandmother, and great-grandmother—during her childhood in California's San Joaquin Valley.

Her grandmother, Jackie says, was a great cook, and everything was made from scratch. "She made her own cheese, my grandfather made his own wine...I grew up with things made. She probably would frown on me buying stuff like salsa verde, but things have changed."

I wish it were possible to get to know Jackie better, but her job as corporate chef for Roy Yamaguchi means she has to keep tabs on his neighbor island restaurants and is pretty much in constant motion.

She does this while being a mom, which I find admirable. I have a hard enough time keeping up with my kids, and I never go anywhere.

Still, Jackie has always been quick to help when I've called about Roy's dishes or her own.

CRAIG T. KOJIMA

She came up with this chile verde dish to contribute to a Fourth of July article in 2002, when I was looking for four special dishes representing America's mixed heritage. This is not a Roy's dish, but something personal for Jackie and I think it says a lot of both her sense of adventure and tradition.

She says traditional chile verde would be prohibitively time-consuming, with the tomatillo-based salsa made first, followed by three hours of cooking time for the meat. So she's taken some shortcuts. "It makes it easier for us to make it more often."

Once you get past blanching the pig's feet and cutting up the pork, the dish does come together simply. As it all simmers on the stove, you can relax.

The meat should get so tender that it falls apart, Jackie said. "It doesn't even resemble feet."

Chile Verde with Pig's Feet

Serves 10

2	pounds pig's feet, cut into sections
2	pounds diced pork butt
1	large onion, diced
¼	cup pork lard or vegetable oil
3	cups chicken stock or broth
21	ounces Herdez® brand salsa verde (see note)
2	jalapeños, diced
3	bay leaves
2	tablespoons dry oregano
5	cloves garlic, smashed
1	tablespoon peppercorns

Place pig's feet in a pot of salted water and bring to a boil. Boil 5 minutes; drain and rinse. Repeat process once.

In a large pot, brown diced pork, onion and lard. Add pig's feet to the pot along with all of the remaining ingredients. Simmer, covered, on medium heat, 2 hours. Stir occasionally, to prevent sticking. Remove cover and simmer another hour to allow liquid to reduce and flavor to intensify.

Debone pig's feet, if desired. Serve with fresh chopped cilantro, lime wedges, and hot fresh tortillas.

Note: Most supermarkets carry the Herdez® brand in the Mexican food section. It comes in 7-ounce cans.

Index

About the author

Betty Shimabukuro is features editor at the *Honolulu Star-Bulletin* and editor of the Food section. "By Request" has been her weekly column since 1998. She came upon the challenge of hunting recipes after many years of news writing and editing—her cooking training involved nothing more than a spotty apprenticeship with her mother, Betty Zane Shimabukuro, a legendary home economist with the University of Hawai'i's Cooperative Extension Service. Shimabukuro is a graduate of the UH journalism program and Kaiser High School (Go, Cougars!). Her desire to work in daily newspapers took her first to Guam, then across the country to Florida, then back again to California. She met her husband, Rob Perez, at her first newspaper job at the *Pacific Daily News* on Guam, and today they have three children who are variously amused and distressed by the experimental dinners that are part of a food writer's home life.